D251 BLOCK 1 UNIT 4
SOCIAL SCIENCES: A SECOND LEVEL COURSE
D251 ISSUES IN DEAFNESS

BEING DEAF

UNIT 4
THE OTHER DEAF COMMUNITY?

PREPARED FOR THE COURSE TEAM BY
GEORGE TAYLOR AND RUKHSANA MFHFRAII

PAINTING ON COVER AND TITLE PAGE BY TREVOR LANDELL

The Open University

THIS COURSE HAS BEEN PRODUCED WITH FUNDING
FROM THE DEPARTMENT OF HEALTH

D251 Core Course Team

ANNE DARBY Diploma Placements Officer, Faculty of Social Sciences

SUSAN GREGORY Senior Lecturer in Psychology, Faculty of Social Sciences (Course Team Chair)

YVONNE HOLMES Secretary, Faculty of Social Sciences

LINDA JANES Course Manager, Faculty of Social Sciences

GEORGE TAYLOR Lecturer in Interdisciplinary Social Sciences, Faculty of Social Sciences

Other Open University Contributors

JULIET BISHOP Research Fellow in Social Sciences, Faculty of Social Sciences

DEBBIE CROUCH Designer

TIM DANT Research Fellow in Health and Social Welfare, Continuing Education

VIC FINKELSTEIN Senior Lecturer in Health and Social Welfare, Continuing Education

GERALD HALES Research Fellow, Institute of Educational Technology

FIONA HARRIS Editor

KEITH HOWARD Graphic Artist

MARY JOHN Senior Lecturer in Psychology, Faculty of Social Sciences

VIC LOCKWOOD BBC Producer

KEN PATTON BBC Producer

ALISON TUCKER BBC Producer

External Consultants

LORNA ALLSOP Centre for Deaf Studies, University of Bristol

LARAINE CALLOW Consultant in Deafness

MARY FIELDER National Council of Social Workers with Deaf People

GILLIAN M. HARTLEY Teacher, Thorn Park School, Bradford

LYNNE HAWCROFT Royal National Institute for the Deaf

JIM KYLE Centre for Deaf Studies, University of Bristol

PADDY LADD London Deaf Video Project

CARLO LAURENZI National Deaf Children's Society

CLIVE MASON Presenter, BBC 'See Hear'

RUKHSANA MEHERALI Educational Psychologist, Royal School for the Deaf, Derby

DOROTHY MILES Writer, Lecturer and Poet

BOB PECKFORD British Deaf Association

CHRISTINE PLAYER Tutor Adviser

SHARON RIDGEWAY National Council of Social Workers with Deaf People

JANICE SILO Teacher of the Deaf, Derbyshire

External Assessors

MARY BRENNAN Co-director, MA and Advanced Diploma in Sign Language Studies, University of Durham

MALCOLM PAYNE Head of Department of Applied Community Studies, Manchester Polytechnic

Sign Language Interpreters

BYRON CAMPBELL

ELIZABETH JONES

KYRA POLLITT

LINDA RICHARDS

The Open University
Walton Hall, Milton Keynes
MK7 6AB

First published 1991

Designed by the Graphic Design Group of the Open University

Printed in the United Kingdom by The Open University

ISBN 0 7492 0050 2

This publication forms part of the Open University course D251 Issues in Deafness. If you have not enrolled on the course and would like to buy this or other Open University material, please write to Open University Educational Enterprises Ltd, 12 Cofferidge Close, Stony Stratford, Milton Keynes MK11 1BY, United Kingdom. If you wish to enquire about enrolling as an Open University student, please write to the Admissions Office, The Open University, P.O. Box 48, Walton Hall, Milton Keynes MK7 6AB, United Kingdom.

Unit 4 The Other Deaf Community?

prepared for the course team by George Taylor and Rukhsana Meherali

Contents

Associated study materials

Reader One, Article 10, 'Making Plans for Nigel: the Erosion of Identity by Mainstreaming', Paddy Ladd.

Reader One, Article 11, 'Life at Secondary School', Elizabeth Craddock.

Reader One, Article 12, 'A Polytechnic with a Difference', Lucy Briggs.

Reader One, Article 19, 'A Deaf Teacher: A Personal Odyssey', Janice Silo.

Reader One, Article 22, 'How I Live with Deaf-Blindness', Patrick Murphy.

Reader One, Article 23, 'A Deaf-Gay Man', David Nyman.

Reader One, Article 24, 'Growing up in Care', Andrew Charles and Rachel Coombs.

Reader One, Article 32, 'Memories of a War', George Taylor.

Reader One, Article 33, 'Memories of a School', George Taylor.

Set Book: D. Miles, *British Sign Language: A Beginner's Guide*, pp. 25–6.

D251 Issues in Deafness

Readers

Reader One: Taylor, G. and Bishop, J. (eds) (1990) *Being Deaf: The Experience of Deafness*, London, Pinter Publishers.

Reader Two: Gregory, S. and Hartley, G.M. (eds) (1990) *Constructing Deafness*, London, Pinter Publishers.

Set Books

Kyle, J. and Woll, B. (1985) *Sign Language: The Study of Deaf People and Their Language*, Cambridge, Cambridge University Press.

Miles, D. (1988) *British Sign Language: A Beginner's Guide,* London, BBC Books (BBC Enterprises). With a chapter by Paddy Ladd.

Videotapes

Aims and objectives

The aims of this unit are:

1   To look at the different groups that constitute the Deaf community.

2   To explore the notion that Deaf people identify themselves as Deaf first, regardless of membership of any other group.

3   To look at how the Deaf community defines acceptability.

4   To identify how the process of marginalization operates in the Deaf community.

5   To raise some of the issues regarded as important by the subject groups identified in the unit.

6   To look at the way in which prejudices in wider society operate in the Deaf community.

By the end of the unit you should:

1   Have an understanding of the major issues which concern the subject groups and be able to relate these to similar issues in society as a whole.

2   Be able to place the current issues of the subject groups into a historical perspective.

3   Have developed an analysis and a theoretical framework which can be applied to a number of different groups both in the Deaf community and in wider society.

Study guide

We advise you *not* to read through the whole unit in one go but to arrange your study in the way we suggest. The subject groups looked at in this unit are very different from each other and the issues are complex. You will find it more satisfactory and easier to engage with the material if you work through the issues raised in each section before moving on.

A suggested plan for study would be:

Week one
Study as far as the end of Section 1.

Try and maintain an awareness of representations of Black people in society and continue to look for the underlying messages.

Week two
Study Section 2 and Section 3.

This stage may be a good opportunity to review the way you are approaching the ITQ on page 7–8 and also the ITQs at the end of each section, and to identify any alterations in your views.

Week three
Study the rest of the unit. Pay particular attention to Activity 4 in the Conclusion—your overall appreciation of the material will be enhanced by the time spent on this activity.

Introduction

This unit will be looking at a number of different groups within the Deaf community; namely, Black deaf people, gay and lesbian deaf people, deaf-blind people, older deaf people and oral deaf people. The approach we have chosen to take is to look at these groups in relation to what many people would consider to be the popular image of the Deaf community: that is, a community made up of white, heterosexual, able-bodied, sign language users. But why is this the popular image? And is it true? If so, how is it constructed, and by what means is it maintained?

Simone de Beauvoir defined this approach when she wrote of the position of women in relation to men:

> ... just as for the ancients there was an absolute vertical with reference to which the oblique was defined, so there is an absolute human type, the masculine ... Thus humanity is male and man defines woman not in herself but as relative to him; she is not regarded as an autonomous being ... She is defined and differentiated with reference to man and not he with reference to her; she is the incidental, the inessential as opposed to the essential. He is the Subject, he is the Absolute—she is the Other.

> (de Beauvoir, 1988)

The 'Absolute', the 'Subject', in this unit is the popular image of the Deaf community, and we make the assumption that this will be most easily found in Deaf clubs throughout the country. The 'Other' we are taking to be the groups listed above. Where they can be found is more problematic, and one of the issues raised in this unit.

The point made by de Beauvoir is that the notion of 'difference' is used as a rationale for an unequal distribution of power; that is, women are seen as, for instance, less capable and less intelligent than men and therefore cannot be trusted with important issues. This notion of the 'Other' can easily be applied in a number of areas: a most obvious example being the way in which British society is constructed around white citizenship, and in which Black people are seen as immigrants who are a threat to British culture (Fryer, 1984). In other words, Black people are not viewed as rightful members of a multi-racial society; rather, they are expected to adapt to a 'British' way of life if they want to live in Britain: they are the 'Other'. Similarly with social class—unless it is accepted that the working classes are intrinsically 'wicked' and 'stupid', and the middle classes intrinsically 'honest' and 'clever', why is it that prisons are populated predominantly by the working classes whereas the overwhelming majority of students at university are middle class?

Within this framework, the 'subject' or 'absolute' is treated as the 'norm', whilst there is a prescribed position for those who do not fit the definition of 'normal'. Wheelchair users, for example, meet this every day because the world is designed around the notion that 'normal' equals 'able-bodied', and any concessions to people who do not walk are at most an afterthought and always in the control of those who are able-bodied. Paulo Freire (1972) described this kind of attitude as 'false generosity'. By expressing this 'generosity', the oppressors attempt to soften at least the outward appearance of their power. However, in order to be in the position of 'benefactor' at all, the oppressors must maintain their position of power and in this way they perpetuate injustice.

We suggest that to deconstruct what is considered 'normal' in the Deaf community would give us these elements: white, heterosexual, able-bodied, sign language user, Deaf club attender. This may not be a surprising list as some of these elements also feature as desirable in the hearing majority. However, being the 'Other' is a position that Deaf people hold in relation to hearing people, and there is a notion that the Deaf community is more closely knit than would ever be considered the case for the hearing community. We interviewed a number of Deaf people when preparing this unit and one of them told us: 'The Deaf community is just like a family really, and all Deaf people are in it'.

So is our suggestion for the constructed image of 'normality' in the Deaf community reasonable? And how does this 'family' of Deaf people relate to those who do not fit the image?

De Beauvoir claims that the establishing of the 'self', the 'subject', the 'one', is *always* accompanied by the setting up of the 'Other' as a hostile and inferior group (de Beauvoir, 1988). Thus, aborigines are 'natives' to colonists; people from another country are 'foreigners'; and to inhabitants of a small village, new residents are seen as 'strangers' and therefore treated with suspicion.

We would therefore expect to find between the different groups in the Deaf community a series of relationships characterized by hostility and opposition. But de Beauvoir claims that the nature of 'Otherness' is not absolute, that it alters in specific circumstances, and that, because the 'Other' consciousness sets up a reciprocal claim to being the 'subject', some negotiation is necessary at certain times. A shift in prevailing social conditions, such as war or major political change, will effect changes in the status of 'Other' groups (Blacks, Jews, Gypsies etc.), except, that is, for women. De Beauvoir identifies the lack of a concrete means of organizing themselves (the absence of a specific women's language, religion or history) as the main reason why women are less able to change their status as the 'Other'.

ITQ
You will be aware by this stage of the course of the importance of language and culture as issues for the Deaf community, but how does this affect the different groups within the Deaf community if the relationship between them is founded on hostility and opposition? Does the language of the Deaf community become the language of the oppressor in relation to the 'Other' groups of Deaf people? And is their status as 'Other' therefore absolute in contrast to de Beauvoir's claim? Or can it be altered by a change in social conditions? Or negotiated in special circumstances because of a reciprocal claim to being the 'subject'?

Ask yourself the following questions about each of the groups looked at in this unit: Black deaf people, gay and lesbian deaf people, deaf-blind people, older deaf people and oral deaf people.

(a) What circumstances maintain the position of these groups as the 'Other'?

(b) How can their position be changed?

(c) How would you describe the nature of the relationship between these groups and the majority group in the Deaf community?

Make a note of the answers you come up with now. We will refer you to these questions again at the end of each section and at the end of the unit. You may find that you alter your view as a result of working in more detail on the issues raised.

It may be helpful to read the first part of this unit again, and also to remind yourself of the issues raised in Unit 2.

We wanted to find out from Deaf people themselves how they viewed their community and the members of it. We interviewed a number of Deaf people in England, both in groups and individually, in the North, the Midlands and the South. The groups we interviewed were: deaf-blind people, Black deaf people, gay and lesbian deaf people, older deaf people, oral deaf people and representative groups from three Deaf clubs.

The groups themselves are all very different from each other in terms of their predominant characteristics and their social status. Although it is theoretically possible for one person to be eligible for membership of more than one group, if not of all of them, this was not reflected in the groups we interviewed. For example, only in the deaf-blind group did we meet deaf-blind people, and, other than in the Black deaf groups, we met only three Black deaf people. We also found that the identity of the individual was consistent with the group identity; for example, Black deaf people in white Deaf groups described themselves as Deaf people who happened to be Black, whereas in the Black deaf groups the participants referred to themselves firstly by their ethnic origin. We will return to this issue later in the unit.

Because the nature of the groups differed in this way, we have not attempted to represent them in a uniform manner. To do so would be to make them fit to a shape of our choosing rather than theirs. Instead, we have been guided by the wishes of the group members themselves as to what they identify as being important for them. Our concern has been with drawing out the issues and making them available for critical exploration. In doing so, we have tried to avoid expressing any kind of 'false generosity'.

Each group was self-selecting, in that all of the individuals within each group wanted to participate. With the exception of one Afro-Caribbean and one Asian group, all of the groups existed prior to our research. We simply made contact and asked if we could interview individuals of the group's choosing. This is an important point, as we did not want to construct a notion of organization within the Deaf community that exists only for the purposes of research. Also, in the group interviews an interpreter appointed by the group was used in order to achieve as high a level of clarity as possible.

We have not, of course, covered all sections of the Deaf community. Any enquiry into the different groups that comprise the Deaf community will almost inevitably be exclusive. We have not attempted to reflect or establish a hierarchy in the groups we have selected, and the analysis we use in this unit can also be applied to other groups, such as deaf women, or deaf people with a mental handicap.

The aim of the interviews was to elicit opinions, attitudes and personal experiences, and we have made no attempt to quantify the information. A number of statements and questions were used as an aid to start a discussion. These concerned the Deaf community, Deaf clubs, teachers, social workers and doctors, and the different groups that took part in the research.

We will look at the different groups in our sphere of interest by focusing first on their 'difference' and then on their relationship with the rest of the Deaf community. In particular, do they consider themselves to be the 'Other'?

Note that in this unit we will be using the term 'Black' to refer to both Afro-Caribbean and Asian people.

1 Black deaf people

With Black hearing people that's OK, but it's hard with white Deaf people; it can be difficult, there is strong feeling there because we're not really quite the same. You feel a bit stronger with Black people really, with white Deaf people it's not the same.

(A Black deaf woman, 1989)

1.1 Black people in Britain

There were Africans in Britain before the English came here.

(Fryer, 1984)

There is a commonly held belief that Black people have only been resident in Britain in any significant numbers since the Second World War. In the 1950s the country was desperately short of unskilled labour for post-war economic revival. As a result, an active recruitment policy was instituted in Commonwealth countries, offering high wages to unskilled workers to work in the iron foundries and cotton mills. Many people in the Commonwealth were encouraged to come and work in the 'mother country'.

Active recruitment of Commonwealth citizens raised the profile of Black people in Britain at this time, but the earliest references to Black residents go back much further than that. In his book *Staying Power*, Peter Fryer maps out the history of Black people in Britain, and identifies the early part of the third century AD as the first attested date for the arrival of Black people in this country: African soldiers formed part of the Imperial Roman army that occupied Britain for three and a half centuries.

Irish chronicles of the ninth century refer to 'Blue Men' being brought to Ireland from Morocco by the Vikings. There is some evidence that Africans were present around the Norfolk area in the tenth century, and from the sixteenth century the records are full of references to Black soldiers, artists, performers, poets and servants, living in Scotland. James IV of Scotland had many Black people in his court. One of them, as well as being a 'favourite' of James, was also the subject of a poem by the Scottish poet William Dunbar. The King himself championed her in the tournaments of 1507, 1508 and 1509, a fact that appalled Sir James Balfour Paul when editing the Third Volume of the Accounts of the Lord High Treasurer of Scotland. Referring to James IV of Scotland, he said: '... he did much to bring into disrepute from his fantastic elevation of a Negress to a position which in the palmy days of chivalry had only been held by the fairest and noblest in the land' (ALHTS III, in Fryer, 1984).

Henry VII and Henry VIII employed at least one Black musician. This man was often referred to as the 'Blacke Trumpet' and is portrayed in the most precious treasure of the College of Arms, a roll depicting the 1511 Westminster Tournament. Although his real name is not known, the treasure of the Chamber records it as 'John Blanke', which is interesting as this means 'John White'.

The first reference to a group of people from Africa coming to England was in 1555. They were brought by John Lok in order to learn English, with a view to their returning to Africa as interpreters to enable the English to carve out a slice of West African trade in ivory, pepper and gold, which until that time had been dominated by the Portuguese. As Fryer points out, they came: '... before we had potatoes, or tobacco, or tea, and nine years before Shakespeare was born' (Fryer, 1984).

The group came from Shama, on the coast of modern-day Ghana. Their stay in England was successful as they were indeed effective in developing trading links with English merchants. Since that time there have been many references in public records to Black people in England.

The first accurate reference to Asian people in Britain is in regard to a Lord Mayor's pageant in the seventeenth century, as performers. There were many references in the eighteenth century to 'Gentoo' and 'Moormen' servants (Hindu and Muslim); these were largely from Bengal and Madras. The English middle classes with the East India Company in India grew accustomed to a high level of personal service and often brought Asian servants back to England with them.

Indian seamen (known as Lascars), stranded in England without pay after employment with the East India Company, were living in England from the 1780s amongst the 'black poor'. Their plight was such that they were described by one concerned observer as: '... miserable objects ... shivering and starting ... a race of human beings, who, though different in colour, religion, and country from ourselves, are still our fellow-creatures, and who have been dragged from their warmer and more hospitable climates by our avarice and ambition' (Fryer, 1984).

Political and professional activity by Asian people dates back to 1830. Raja Rammohan Roy, a journalist, philosopher and poet living in London from 1830 to 1833, was the first Indian to make a submission to a parliamentary committee on Indian affairs. This work was continued by Dwarkanath Tagore (grandfather of the celebrated Bengali poet Rabindranath Tagore). Together they formed the British India Society in 1839.

The first Black member of Parliament was Dadabhai Naoroji in 1892, a Liberal MP for Central Finsbury, soon to be followed in 1895 by Sir Mancherjee Merwangee Bhownagree, a Conservative MP for Bethnal Green North East. There were a number of other professional Asian people practising as lecturers, lawyers and scientists, as well as other parliamentary candidates.

The history of Black people, particularly in Britain, is a hidden history. Clearly they have not arrived only recently, they have lived in Britain for centuries, and, in order to understand their situation in Britain today, the historical context must be established. Black deaf people share a cultural history with both Black people and Deaf people—the histories of both these groups are characterized by oppression and by being cast into the role of the 'Other'.

◄ Activity 1

Pause for a moment now and consider some of the points raised so far in Section 1.1, and in particular:

(a) The history of Black people in Britain is hidden.

(b) The histories of Black people and Deaf people are characterized by oppression.

Do you think the situation in contemporary Britain has improved in the way that Black people and Deaf people are popularly represented? Collect a week's supply of a particular national or local daily newspaper and search through for references to Black people and Deaf people. Do you consider the amount of coverage adequate? How many negative (e.g. patronizing, tokenistic, biased) images are there? ◄

◄ Comment

You will probably find that many of the references to Black people and Deaf people in your chosen newspaper are generally negative, in that they are patronizing or they portray their subject as a problem. In attempting to understand the social position of a Black deaf person it is important to analyse the 'messages' that exist in society about Black people and Deaf people. To be Black and Deaf is not simply to have twice as many negative messages because sometimes the messages may conflict with each other. This point will be raised again in Unit 6. ◄

◄ Reading

Now read Article 24 'Growing up in Care' by Andrew Charles and Rachel Coombs in Reader One. Andrew Charles describes his childhood as a Black deaf person in a white hearing foster family. Before you read the article, make a note of the areas you think should be given particular attention in these circumstances in order to ensure that the Black deaf child's social and cultural needs are met. ◄

1.2 Racism in Britain

Errol Lawrence in *The Empire Strikes Back* (Centre for Contemporary Cultural Studies, 1982) establishes the context within which a discussion on racism can be held by saying what racism is not. It is not the same as prejudice, for instance; it is not the inevitable product of something called 'human nature'; and it is not a relic of an imperial past. Fryer reinforces this idea when he states that: 'The primary functions of race prejudice are cultural and psychological. The primary functions of racism are economic and political' (Fryer, 1984).

Race prejudice, according to Fryer, is scrappy and self-contradictory, and is 'orally'[1] transmitted. Racism, on the other hand, is relatively systematic and internally consistent, almost scientific, and is transmitted by the written word. The spark for this pseudo-scientific system (racism) was the interdependence between the English slave trade, sugar plantations and manufacturing industries. The profits available from this arrangement propelled England into a dominant position in world markets in the eighteenth and nineteenth centuries.

Race prejudice, as opposed to racism, however, dates back much earlier. Fryer (1984) cites Pliny the Elder, AD 23 to AD 79, and his description of Africa and Africans in *A Summarie of the Antiquities, and Wonder of the Worlde*. Whilst this was written in the first century AD, it was not published in English until 1566. In this work Pliny weaves reality and fantasy together when he talks of Africans going about without clothes, of some making no marriages and others eating the flesh of panthers and lions. He states that some had no noses, tongues or mouths, that some were ruled by a dog, others had heads like dogs, yet others had no heads at all but eyes and mouths in their breasts. He also referred to their sexual practices as resembling those of animals. This firmly placed the notion in the heads of sixteenth century English people that Africans were lascivious, idle and base creatures.

Darkness as a symbol of danger, evil and fear, and light as a symbol of goodness, safety and purity, are recurrent themes in many cultures, particularly in Western Europe. So use of the words 'Black' and 'White' already had considerable significance before English people 'discovered' Black people. It was then an easy step to cast the Black person as a product of the Devil.

In the Bible, Ham, son of Noah, was cursed for 'discovering' his father's nakedness, banished to hot countries and condemned to be unlucky; his progeny would also be condemned to serve others. The Dutch Reform Church asserted that the reason Ham was cursed in this way was that he had had sexual relations with his wife during 'The Flood', a practice that was strictly forbidden. For this act his offspring would be 'Black'. This is one of the elements that underpins the system of apartheid in South Africa.

Both these descriptions of the origins of Black people have as their basis sexual misconduct, and references to the Devil's influence. And this link is further reinforced in New Testament references to the Devil as 'The Black One' (Epistle of Barnabas), and St Jerome, in the fourth century, said: 'Born of the Devil, we are Black'.

By the time that Shakespeare was writing *Othello*, the notion that Black men were 'sexually dangerous' was taken for granted. Desdemona was described to her father as being '... in the gross clasp of a lascivious Moor' (*Othello*, Act 1, Scene 1). Othello is also referred to in the play as 'A Barbary horse',

---

[1] A broad definition of this concept refers to transmission through stories, jokes, popular songs and face-to-face communication etc. and *not* through the written word. It would therefore also apply to the Deaf community using sign language.

and 'the Devil'. Even though he was a Christian of noble birth, the audiences of the day were not surprised by descriptions of evil and lascivious behaviour. These ideas still hold currency in Western society—the Black man is often portrayed in popular fiction as the 'Sexually Dangerous Other'. The 1970s Hollywood film *Shaft* is one example; Dr Aziz in E.M. Forster's *A Passage to India* is another.

◀ Activity 2
Think back to the time you first became aware of differences between Black people and white people. Make a note of some of the opinions you held about (a) Black people, and (b) white people. Do you consider these to be stereotyped images? And has anything happened to reinforce or change these opinions? ◀

◀ Comment
There are no 'right' or 'wrong' answers here. As children growing up we accumulate a tremendous amount of what we consider to be 'knowledge'. You may find that you hold opinions that you have never questioned simply because they have been with you for a long time. ◀

1.3 Slavery

The earliest known English slaver was Sir John Hawkyns who, in 1562, was the first to embark upon the voyage that came to be known as the 'Golden Triangle'. (There are references to the men brought over from Shama a few years earlier in 1555 by John Lok as being slaves—however, whilst their

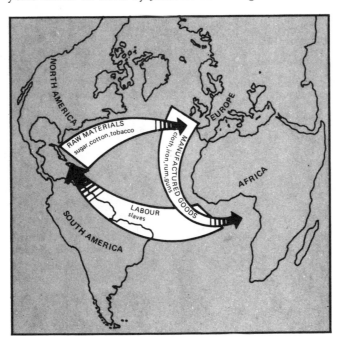

Figure 4.1 The 'Golden Triangle'
(Source: Institute of Race Relations, 1982a)

13

Figure 4.2 Hawkins' coat of arms (Source: Institute of Race Relations, 1982b)

status may not have been that of free men, they were not 'bought and paid for' slaves.) On this voyage, gifts and trinkets were taken from England to Africa, slaves from Africa to the West Indies, and spices and sugar from the West Indies back to England. Sir John Hawkyns' first 'cargo' comprised approximately 300 slaves from Guinea to Haiti. His subsequent voyages were sanctioned by Queen Elizabeth I, and from then on the slave trade from England began in earnest. He was rewarded by being allowed to augment his coat of arms with a bound slave.

Other European countries such as Spain, Portugal and the Netherlands were already active in slavery, and the concept of the subjugated 'Black' was well embedded within English culture—the next step to a formalized slave trade was therefore easily taken.

The bulk of the English slave trade was managed through the ports of London, Bristol and Liverpool, and the wealth of these cities was considerably enhanced by this trade. In fact, without the related trades of slaves and sugar, Bristol and Liverpool would have been no more than minor sea-ports. Despite the significant influence of the slave trade on the development of the City of Liverpool, a 515-page history of the city, written in 1957, and sponsored by the city council, relegates the slave trade to 28 lines. It concludes: 'In the long run, the triangular operation based on Liverpool was to bring benefits to all, not least to the transplanted slaves, whose descendants have subsequently achieved in the New World standards of education and civilization far ahead of their compatriots whom they left behind' (Chandler, 1957, in Fryer, 1984).

These 'benefits' can be measured by some of the treatment regularly doled out to slaves. There are many references to Black people being thrown alive overboard to drown because the slavers could claim compensation from insurance companies for 'lost cargo', whereas any slave who died on board ship was a loss to the slaver. The Solicitor General, John Lee, in 1781, defended this activity as being a simple case of 'goods and chattels' and not of people (Fryer, 1984).

Black people as merchandise to be bought and disposed of by white people is a theme that pervades from the sixteenth century onwards. There are also many instances in which legal judgements were made about Black people being left as property in wills or as the objects of insurance claims, for instance, and about disputes over their ownership. These judgements are characterized by the taken-for-granted right of white people to own Black people.

In the eighteenth century there were many advertisements in English cities offering Black people for sale. These auctions were often conducted in coffee houses and taverns, and no differentiation was made between selling Black people and selling goods and property, as this advertisement from 1757 illustrates: 'For Sale. Ten pipes of raisin wine, a parcel of bottled cyder, and a negro boy' (Fryer, 1984). Often, the person concerned was available in local shops and taverns to be viewed and inspected by prospective purchasers prior to the auction. Clearly, a respect for the dignity of human life was not part of this process.

Slavery was officially ended by the 1833 Abolition of Slavery Act, although the majority of slaves in Britain had by that time freed themselves by escaping from their masters. Black people were used almost exclusively as domestic slaves, and as social opinion turned against this practice it became less desirable or possible to recapture 'runaways'. The debates over abolition

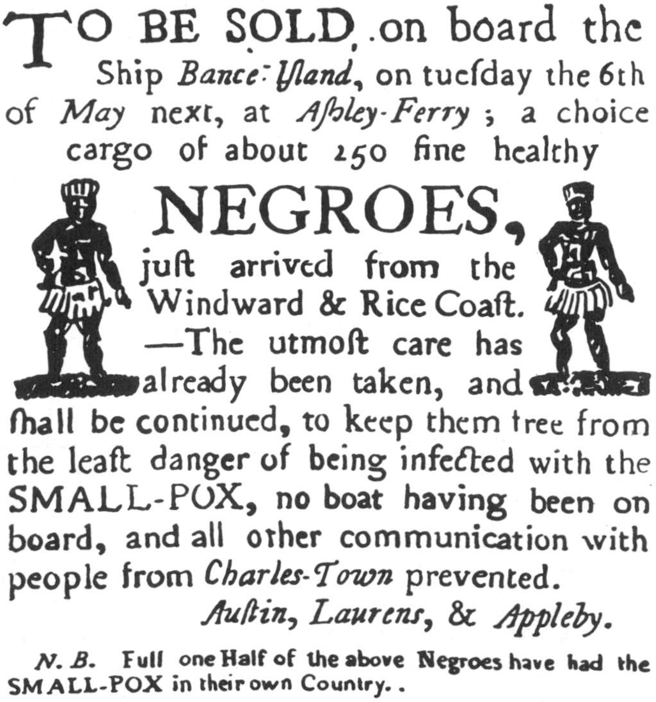

Figure 4.3 Advertisement for sale of 'negroes' (*sic*)
(Source: courtesy of the Mansell Collection)

had raged for many years, with abolitionists demanding immediate cessation of the slave trade, and plantation owners defending it, saying that the wealth and prosperity of Britain relied upon slavery. As early as 1727, the Church of England had defined the parameters of its ministry: 'Christianity and the embracing of the Gospel does not make the least difference in civil property' (Thomas Sherlock, Bishop of Bangor, Salisbury and London, 1727, in Fryer, 1984).

1.4 Racism in the Deaf community

Anderson and Bowe (1972) comment that the issues faced by Black deaf people have been overlooked by almost everyone. They point to a severe lack of integration between Black deaf people and white deaf people, the manifestations of racism within the Deaf community are across a broad range of areas. Anderson and Bowe quote from an article by George Ayers in the US *Journal of Rehabilitation*: 'Many whites fail to recognize, much less accept, the fact that racist attitudes have been institutionalized and transmitted generation to generation amongst their people. They can't see that forms of racism have ranged from unconscious to overt, benign to malignant' (Ayers, 1970, in Anderson and Bowe, 1972).[2]

[2] In our search for material that discusses racism in the Deaf community, we could find nothing more recent than Anderson and Bowe (1972). There may be other writings that we have overlooked but we feel that our difficulty generally in finding material substantiates the claim that this issue is not being addressed, particularly in Britain.

Anderson and Bowe argue that racism is reinforced in schools for deaf children, because Black deaf pupils learn very little about themselves, and the dominating image within pedagogic materials is that of white middle class supremacy. Can we honestly say that the situation is any better in Britain? Where notions of a pluralist society are only very recent in education, and where multicultural issues are covered at all, it is often in a tokenistic fashion. Special education for deaf children in Britain focuses on literacy and numeracy skills to the detriment of developing positive self-images amongst pupils.

1.5 On being like 'us'

A lack of positive role models for Black deaf children in schools, combined with the low expectations of some teachers, compound the effects of deafness and result in low self-esteem and underachievement in Black deaf pupils. Their entry into adult Deaf society is therefore made problematic because their role in the white Deaf community is unclear, and they are often rejected.

White deaf people who are also a product of the same education system will inevitably absorb a white British version of such subjects as history and literature, together with a Eurocentric view of the world. It would be surprising, therefore, if they were to demonstrate high levels of tolerance to Black people in the Deaf community. Most of the white Deaf people that we interviewed claimed not to have any racist views. They were prepared to accept Black people into their clubs, but they expected Black people to adapt their lifestyles, language and culture to be more acceptable to the white Deaf community:

> If they adopt the English way of life, and are prepared to be friendly, they would be OK.
>
> (A white Deaf woman, 1989)

> If anyone comes from abroad they must learn our English language and way of life.
>
> (A white Deaf man, 1989)

> You come across people who are Indians or Pakistanis, they want to run their own communities, don't they? They want to run it themselves. But I don't see why they should have separate schools for their children, they should all learn the same language and it would cut out a lot of racism if everyone went to the same school. They should also be spread around the town and not live together; it would be lot better. If you have them all together they are bound to get into a community and want to go against other people.
>
> (A white Deaf man, 1989)

> They should follow English, they should all follow the English way of life.
>
> (A white Deaf man, 1989)

> If Black people want to live in this country they must accept our laws and way of life.
>
> (A white Deaf man, 1989)

1.6 On being 'themselves'

The notion that Black people have a right to maintain their ethnic cultures in Britain, alongside the dominant white culture, was also largely rejected by the Deaf people we interviewed:

> The trouble is caused by them speaking their own language, there could come a time when an English person misunderstands and thinks it is against them and that causes trouble. It would be better if they could mix in the community and not stay segregated.
>
> (A white Deaf man, 1989)

> If they go to school and they speak their own language and then they meet somebody from another school they are not going to be able to communicate.
>
> (A white Deaf man, 1989)

> If they want something separate, that could cause conflict and it would create problems for them.
>
> (A white Deaf woman, 1989)

Not only were barriers placed in the way of Black Deaf people joining the Deaf community, the white Deaf people we interviewed were prescriptive about how all Black people should lead their lives.

1.7 On being part of the Deaf community

Black Deaf people we interviewed had two very different perspectives on being part of the Deaf community—these were closely related to whether they were Asian or Afro-Caribbean. The Afro-Caribbean Deaf people we interviewed appeared to move more freely between their ethnic community and the Deaf community. The difficulties described to us by Black Deaf people were about having to resist racial abuse and stereotyping. They expressed a wish to be with other Deaf people, which often involved them in compromising their ethnic identity in an attempt to 'fit in'. Despite strenuous efforts to be accepted by the white Deaf community, they frequently found themselves banned from the Deaf club.

> White people, if they get a bit depressed they can get really pushy, and you have to be really firm with them and stand up for yourself.
>
> (A Black Deaf man, 1989)

> Say if I go into the Deaf club and maybe someone starts making a bit of trouble you have to say 'what do you want to cause trouble for? ... they have a different culture and that can create problems.
>
> (A Black Deaf man, 1989)

> Well, Black Deaf people, you can have a strong relationship with a Black Deaf person, but not so much with a white Deaf person, because it can be bit like, you have to push hard, you have to stand up for yourself and fight back with white people.
>
> (A Black Deaf man, 1989)

> I try and learn from other Black Deaf people to be strong. It's difficult sometimes to sort of be in the white Deaf community and you have to learn how to be very strong.
>
> (A Black Deaf man, 1989)

Their experience of racism was the same whether they were with white hearing people or white Deaf people. They drew their strength from other Black people, particularly Black deaf people. Their frustration stemmed from their wish to be more closely embraced by the Deaf community and the resistance with which their efforts were met.

Hairston and Smith (1983) state in their book *Black and Deaf in America* that Black deaf people seldom socialize with white deaf people, preferring to stay with 'their own'. They identify Black deaf clubs that have been in existence for many years, and comment that Black leaders establish these clubs in response to the desires of local Black deaf people.

Segregation, according to Hairston and Smith, sometimes occurs by mutual consent, and they name two Deaf clubs in Washington DC where this has happened. The clubs are twelve blocks apart and have open membership, yet the membership of one is predominantly Black, the other white, and there is no attempt to integrate. Race, and not deafness, claim Hairston and Smith, is the real binding factor.

> It is often said that no two people are alike and it has, in fact, virtually become a universal truth. It is also widely said that no two deaf people are alike—we are all different. However, by the same token we conclude that deafness has the same effect on a person, despite racial, ethnic, or cultural background, but where Black deaf persons are concerned, the differentiating factor lies in being Black rather than in being deaf.
>
> (Hairston and Smith, 1983)

When we interviewed Asian Deaf people, however, we were presented with a different set of issues. Whilst being aware of, and affected by, racism, their major concern centred around certain constraints placed upon them by their families and ethnic communities.

> I know six or seven different friends who really like to come to the club; they'd like to come regularly. I've tried to sort of welcome people, invite them to come in, but they have to stay at home.
>
> (An Asian Deaf man, 1989)

> I tell them that I go to the Deaf club and say, 'Why don't you come to the deaf club?' or, 'Why don't you take your wife to the Deaf club if she's deaf?' and they say, 'No, no, she is staying here'.
>
> (An Asian Deaf man, 1989)

The interviews we conducted with Asian Deaf people revealed clearly defined differences between men and women in the amount of contact they were able to have with other deaf people. Either deaf women were not allowed to go to the Deaf club at all, or they were closely chaperoned by male family members. In one of the interview groups, one of the Asian Deaf women was brought by her husband who insisted on speaking for her and reinterpreting our questions in spoken Gujerati—this despite the fact that she was an able sign language user. It transpired that she had not seen another Deaf person for 4 years.

The restrictions imposed upon deaf Asian women are consistent with the constraints placed upon hearing Asian women. Little consideration was given to their need to mix with other deaf people.

> I've got two sisters and the family are really strongly controlling them, they are very strict over the religious laws. My sister asked if she could go out to see her friends from school and they said, 'No you can't do that, it's not safe enough for you to go outside'. So my sister was really depressed.
>
> (An Asian Deaf man, 1989)

> It's different with Asian people really, it's all right for the boys, but for the girls …
>
> (An Asian Deaf woman, 1989)

Family 'izzat' is the most important value in many Asian families. ('Izzat' is the Urdu word for honour or esteem. The notion of izzat is cross-cultural but Hindi or Punjabi words may be used in different Asian communities.) The loss of izzat affects the whole family group and is thus feared. Unchaperoned girls or women who are seen out by themselves are in danger of being labelled as 'loose' women or out of control of their elders. This may affect their marriage prospects, and also those of other family members.

Figure 4.4 Black deaf people in conversation
(Source: courtesy of the British Deaf Association)

Married women in Asian communities are also bound by child-care responsibilities and household duties. Some are unable to go out at all, whilst others are closely chaperoned and are only allowed to spend a limited time away from their homes.

> They come from seven 'til about nine. They have to go home. Their husbands are very strict, they pick them up because they've got to go home and look after the children.
>
> (An Asian Deaf woman, 1989)

Child-care and household responsibilities also limit the freedom of many white women. You will remember from the discussion in Unit 2 that there is a high incidence of Deaf people marrying other Deaf people. Many Deaf people meet their marriage partners in schools, colleges and Deaf clubs. The difference for Asian deaf women is that the concept of a Deaf community and a Deaf language is not established in Asian cultures. Marriage partners in Asian communities are usually sought amongst the wider community within a socio-economic group. Deafness may not be considered a relevant factor in such arrangements, and many deaf Asian people are married to hearing partners. Deaf Asian people may therefore find themselves linguistically isolated within a large extended family with no access to sign language.

An Asian Deaf contributor to a seminar on 'Deaf People from Ethnic Minority Groups' held in Birmingham in 1989, commented:

> ... the deaf girls were confused and isolated within their culture and it was expected that a husband would be chosen for them and they would be married off. Many of the girls expressed a wish to be married to deaf men but this was refused.

A more general barrier to Asian deaf people mixing with other deaf people is that the idea of a 'social club' is not part of the established structure of Asian social life. Visiting at home, or at the mosque or temple, is the norm, and even within these situations it is usual for people to remain within circles of 'known' others.

> The Asian community, they go and visit each other ... in their houses for hours and hours, and I want to go and communicate with the Deaf community and they say, 'No, it's important you must stay with the hearing friends'.
>
> (An Asian Deaf man, 1989)

1.8 Discussion

The issues affecting Afro-Caribbean deaf people are different from those affecting Asian deaf people. Both groups experience racism but it manifests itself in a different form for each group.

Deafness in Asian communities is seen as a handicap, a weakness, a deficiency. The person with the handicap is therefore viewed as someone who is not 'fully functioning' and may be treated as 'sick'. Decisions regarding that person's life may be taken by other members of the family; this applies particularly to important decisions that have implications for the future. Thus, a deaf individual may not be included in the process of decision making, even when the decision may have profound, or long-term, effects on that individual's life.

Asian cultures stress the notion and importance of 'the family', and a sense of self-worth is rooted in the strength of the family. The presence of a deaf person in the family reflects upon the whole group, and it can become the cause of self-examination: Why is that person deaf? Is God angry? Have we sinned? Attempts may be made for atonement by offering special prayers or treatments:

> They used to give me those little sweet things, it was actually rose petals with some sort of special water that they had mixed with it, and I'd have to eat this and swallow it right down, and I said, 'If I swallow this it will kill me'. And they said, 'No, no God has given you this and God might make you hearing if you eat it'.
>
> (An Asian Deaf man, 1989)

In Deaf clubs individual differences are likely to be obscured, not only between Asian and Afro-Caribbean, but also between individuals in each group. Black people represent their stereotypes and are given little opportunity to express their own uniqueness. Some of the myths that surround Afro-Caribbean people include their love of music, their sense of rhythm, and their sporting prowess. We also found this reflected in their involvement in Deaf clubs, where they were often included in sports teams but seldom in decision-making forums. American writers, Anderson and Bowe (1972) and Hairston and Smith (1983) also comment on this.

In one of the clubs we visited, Black Deaf people formed more than 50 per cent of the membership, and it was openly stated that without their support the club would not be viable. Despite this, the groups selected to represent the club were exclusively white.

Although Afro-Caribbean and Asian deaf people are equally cast into the role of the 'Other' in the Deaf community, they do not actually comprise a cohesive Black group with a shared identity. The oppression that Black people have to struggle against has the effect of separating them from each other, and from potential support, as well as from the white Deaf community.

ITQ
Now return to the questions we asked you in the first ITQ on page 7–8.

Would you answer the questions in the same way now in respect of Black deaf people? If not, try to identify what it is that has caused you to alter your view. If your answers are broadly similar to those you came up with at the beginning, try and think of some new information which you have now, but did not have at the beginning, or some facet of the debate which you had not taken into account. Make some notes and keep them for Activity 4 at the end of this unit.

---

2 Gay and lesbian deaf people

They are afraid because we are different and therefore not acceptable. They think what we do is wrong, but they don't know us, and we get the blame for their fear of the unknown.

(A gay Deaf man, 1989)

2.1 Homosexuality, religion and the law

Since Biblical times, non-procreative sex, particularly sex between men, has been regarded as dangerous to the stability of Judeo-Christian society.

If anyone lie with a man as with a woman, both have committed an abomination, let them be put to death: their blood be upon them.

(*Leviticus*, 20:13)

Moran (in Shepherd and Wallis, 1989) develops this theme. The medieval Church's view of sodomy as an act between men was informed through an understanding of 'Man's' relationship with God. To be sodomite was to be without God, to be possessed by the Devil, to be evil, impure, unclean, diseased, irrational, unnatural, animal, and of course, womanly. These qualities, being the antithesis of 'Godliness', serve to ally the sodomite with the Devil, thus producing a violent separation between God and the Devil, and locating homosexuals in the low, inferior, condemned, the 'Other' category.

◀ Reading
Now read Article 23 'A Deaf-Gay Man' by David Nyman in Reader One. David Nyman is a Deaf gay man, and in the article he describes his 'coming out' and the way he feels he must be careful in managing his social encounters. ◀

Figure 4.5   Gay men and lesbians campaigning
(Source: courtesy of Brenda Prince, Format)

The earliest reference to homosexuality in a legal statute in Britain was in the 1533 Act of Henry VIII, in which the same language was adopted to describe homosexual acts as unnatural. The penalty for the 'Abominable Vice of Buggery' was death. Lesbianism, as is usual in criminal codes throughout history, was ignored. The law remained virtually unchanged until the 1885 Criminal Law Amendment Act on prostitution, vagrancy and homosexuality. (This is commonly known as the Labouchere Amendment.) This Act made homosexual acts illegal, whether in public or in private, and became known as 'The Blackmailers' Charter'. In 1810, the death penalty was imposed in 80 per cent of cases for homosexuality, but in only 25 per cent of cases for other 'capital' offences (Weeks, 1977).

In the modern, scientific world, where the medical profession has largely replaced the clergy in the role of disseminators of 'wisdom', the language used to describe homosexuality is medico-scientific, but still informed by medieval concepts! Homosexual man (sic) is seen as a biological mistake, a quirk of evolution, a mismanaged developmental stage, the 'Other' in nature. Heterosexuality is the norm, the 'healthy', homosexuality the violent antithesis, the abnormal, the 'unhealthy'. Both the religious and the medical languages construct an image of 'Extreme Otherness' which is then legitimated in legal statute. In law the definition of homosexuality is that of danger, 'The Dangerous Other' (Moran, in Shepherd and Wallis, 1989).

The 1967 Sexual Offences Act loosened slightly the law regarding homosexual practice, by decriminalizing sexual acts in private between consenting men over the age of 21. Surveillance continues in the public domain.

The edges between the public and the private domains are often blurred, however. The Deaf community has a reputation for being a community where news spreads very quickly, and gay and lesbian people still feel the need to conceal their sexual orientation for fear of being ostracized. This fear is borne out by the experiences of some gay Deaf people.

> I was a committee member of my local Deaf club, I was married at the time. No one at the Deaf club knew about my being gay. When I 'came out' I separated from my wife, she told people at the Deaf club and everyone there started abusing me, they all had a very bad attitude towards me as a gay person. One day some of them came to my house and beat me up … I don't want any more to do with the Deaf club because of their attitude towards me and the abuse I suffered.
>
> (A gay Deaf man, 1989)

In our interviews with Deaf people around the country no questions met with such an extreme reaction from heterosexual Deaf people as those we asked about gay and lesbian people. The feelings expressed ranged from unwillingness to discuss the subject to absolute disgust and horror.

> It's like a sickness to me. I do not like to discuss this subject.
>
> (A Deaf man, 1989)

> Shocking, it's shocking. Both homosexuals and lesbians are really shocking and the government just allows them. They want clubs open for gays and I am really surprised. I've seen them and it makes me feel sick. Men kissing each other, and women kissing each other … urrgh!
>
> (A Deaf woman, 1989)

2.2 Myths and fears

In this section we will look at some of the beliefs that were commonly held amongst those deaf people we interviewed and which construct and maintain the stereotypical view of gay and lesbian people. We will use quotations to illustrate.

Why do you think people become homosexual?

Don't know! Perhaps men become gay because girls just don't want them and they decide to go with a man. Perhaps a lesbian thinks that a man doesn't want her and goes with another girl.

(A Deaf woman, 1989)

The family can pass it on.

(A Deaf woman, 1989)

Some people can be born that way, half male, half female. The genes in their body can be that way. Also the way they are brought up. If they are male they can be treated as if they are female.

(A Deaf woman, 1989)

Figure 4.6 'Pride and prejudice'
(Source: courtesy of Ray Hamilton, Camera Press)

... maybe they were encouraged when they were younger by another man. Their parents don't know, they make love and when they grow up they don't want a woman, they prefer another man.

(A Deaf man, 1989)

Maybe if they were married, got divorced ... the woman thinks 'never again', then she goes and finds another woman, that's why she's gay.

(A Deaf man, 1989)

Say there's a gay man, maybe he teaches his son to be gay and takes him to clubs, that sort of thing. I've heard a lot about clubs where they are all men and maybe the son would learn being gay from there.

(A Deaf man, 1989)

 ◀ Activity 3
Make a note of what you consider to be the main reasons as to why some people are homosexual. Ask amongst your family or friends, or other people with whom you usually mix. Is there a consistent view? ◀

In our interviews and informal discussions there was a high level of confusion over the reason as to why some people are homosexual. The most commonly held view, which was also expressed by gay and lesbian deaf people themselves, was that segregated schooling reduces the opportunities for forming heterosexual relationships and therefore encourages homosexuality:

I think one of the reasons is because we went to residential schools, boys only and girls only.

(A gay Deaf man, 1989)

I agree with that. I went to a mixed boarding school, but we were kept separate from the boys. Quite a number of the girls I went to school with experimented sexually with each other and did not see anything wrong with that. It was only later I discovered that what we were doing was supposed to be wrong. I found out afterwards that in the boys' school they were doing the same.

(A Deaf lesbian, 1989)

My school is known as the gay school because such a high proportion of the pupils there are gay ... I have no regrets.

(A gay Deaf man, 1989)

Babuscio (1988) refers to the Kinsey formulation which concludes that all mammals have the capacity to respond to any sufficient stimulus, and that the conditioning effects of the first sexual encounter and the indirect but powerful conditioning of social codes will influence a person's sexual choice. Although the views about residential schools would at first appear to be rather naïve, there can be little doubt that segregated residential education for deaf children may be a significant factor in the development of the gay Deaf community. Many writers in the field (themselves gay or lesbian) see little mileage in looking for causes, and prefer to concentrate on developing political awareness and the acceptance of a gay and lesbian life-style within a pluralist society (Weeks, 1977; Clark, 1987; Babuscio, 1988; Moran, in Shepherd and Wallis, 1989).

2.3 Homosexuals and children

Many of the Deaf people we interviewed considered gay and lesbian people to be a threat to children:

> ... we don't want a bad example to be set to others, especially the children, especially if they see what is going on here.
>
> (A Deaf woman, 1989)

> I am against it when it can affect the children of homosexual people. I can't agree with that for the sake of the child.
>
> (A Deaf man, 1989)

> ... it's in the blood, if there is a gay man he may well abuse children. There's a problem there, it's a difficult situation.
>
> (A Deaf man, 1989)

> Gay men or lesbian women would have no interest in children and they are only interested in their own relationships. But then you've got the problem then with bisexual people and there is a danger there.
>
> (A Deaf woman, 1989)

One Deaf woman closely associated gay men with sexual offences against children such as kidnapping for sex, keeping young girls prisoner for sexual purposes and for pornographic films. The tabloid press was often quoted by the heterosexual Deaf people we interviewed as their only source of information about the activities of gay and lesbian people, whereas the Deaf gay and lesbian groups gained their information from a wider variety of sources, including the 'quality press', books, and articles in journals.

Heterosexual Deaf people we interviewed consistently put gay and lesbian Deaf people in the role of 'Dangerous Other', although none could think of an incident to support his or her strongly held convictions.

Gay and lesbian Deaf people we interviewed were aware of the suspicion in which they were held:

> There are a lot of children being beaten and battered by their mothers and fathers so I think it is unfair to level that accusation at gays.
>
> (A Deaf lesbian, 1989)

> I have read quite a lot about how straight people are more dangerous to children than gay people. When you read about children being physically and sexually abused it is more often by straight people than gay people.
>
> (A gay Deaf man, 1989)

Bancroft, writing in the *British Medical Journal*, comments that:

> Illness can be manifested as sexual behaviour but such behaviour is more likely to be heterosexual than homosexual.
>
> (Bancroft, 1988)

2.4 Transexual/transvestite

Another commonly held view expressed by the Deaf people we interviewed was that gay and lesbian people often cross-dressed and took on the characteristics associated with the opposite sex. Notions of gender, sexual behaviour and sex roles were often conflated:

> The problem is if they're gay, you look at somebody and think she is a beautiful woman, all dressed up with a man, and really it's not a woman it's another man, both men together. But from the back she looks lovely, they're both gay, the man and the woman. I've seen quite a lot.
>
> (A Deaf woman, 1989)

> ... say if I was a man and I wanted to find a new girlfriend and failed and failed and failed, then perhaps I might actually try and dress up as a woman or something and become gay.
>
> (A Deaf man, 1989)

The first person to separate transvestism from homosexuality was Hirschfeld in 1910 (in Weeks, 1983). The popular view of the cross-dressing homosexual is long established and can be seen in the pejorative language used to describe male homosexuals—for example, Nancy-boy, Marianne and Molly. And this was certainly reflected in the views of the Deaf people we interviewed. 'Political Drag' was a device used by some gay communities in the 1970s, not to try and be female but to reject the strait-jacket of being stereotypically male.

Gough (in Shepherd and Wallis, 1989) describes the conscious shift in image adopted by many gay communities, away from 'limp wrists' and 'foppish' mannerisms to images of gay men constructed around male physiology. To be effective as a 'leatherman/biker', a 'cowboy', or a 'construction worker', or one of the many styles adopted by the gay community, meant many hours in the gym developing an athletic male physique.

2.5 How AIDS affects the Deaf community

We were initially very cautious about discussing AIDS within the context of the homosexual community because of the way that the homosexual community has been blamed for its rapid spread. However, when we interviewed gay and lesbian Deaf people they impressed upon us the importance of including a section on AIDS. In their opinion:

1 A disproportionate number of deaf people are HIV positive.
2 Access to information on AIDS is difficult for deaf people—information and discussion are consequently limited.

> It's their own fault if they catch AIDS. They should go to the doctor; they might get VD. I'm not going to help them, no. A lot of them just don't care, then they get worse and it spreads, AIDS will spread.
>
> (A Deaf woman, 1989)

I don't think they are right, and it is causing a lot of AIDS. I think they should pay for their own hospital treatment and not put a strain on the NHS, because that is where a lot of NHS money is going to. If they want to carry on like that they should pay for their treatment. They should have some insurance to pay for it.

(A Deaf man, 1989)

I think it's awful because gay and lesbians ... I mean really through gay people because of that AIDS is spreading and spreading and children and babies may be catching it because of that. I really think it's awful the stuff I've seen in the newspapers.

(A Deaf woman, 1989)

Watney (in Shepherd and Wallis, 1989) refers to the research undertaken by Professor Michael Adler which concludes that: 'The commonest mode of transmission [of AIDS] throughout the world is by sexual intercourse. Whether this is anal or vaginal is unimportant' (Shepherd and Wallis, 1989).

The division of people into high-risk and low-risk groups obfuscates this evidence and leads many to conclude that homosexual acts are primarily responsible for the transmission of the HIV virus.

Whilst factual information about the incidence of AIDS in the Deaf community was lacking amongst the Deaf people we interviewed, the gay Deaf community had very strong opinions about the position:

There are several Deaf people, gays and straights, who have acquired AIDS. To date sixteen people have acquired AIDS, and nine have died from it. There are over thirty people who are HIV positive and they are from a cross-section of the Deaf community. There is a higher incidence of AIDS in the Deaf community than in the hearing community, perhaps because the Deaf community is smaller and it spreads more quickly.

(A Deaf lesbian, 1989)

The responses from Deaf gays and lesbians towards AIDS has been very good, similar to hearing gays and lesbians.

(A Deaf lesbian, 1989)

I know people who have died; we have a lot of friends who have AIDS and we always support them and care for them—whereas the straight Deaf community rejects them. This has happened a number of times.

(A gay Deaf man, 1989)

The popular press tends to reinforce the view that heterosexuals are not responsible for the spread of AIDS. Babuscio (1988) maintains that, according to the media and sometimes the medical profession, 'homosexual promiscuity' is to blame for the spread of AIDS. In other words, the lifestyle of gay men, rather than a specific organism, is the culprit. Drug users are categorized in the same way, and, as AIDS is alleged to have originated in Central Africa, so are African people. In this sense they are all consigned to the role of 'Dangerous Other', and thus become symbols of the ultimate danger, death: 'It is the same sort of attitude you would have towards a murderer' (A gay Deaf man, 1989).

2.6 In the Deaf community
2.6.1 Behaviour

> I am always on my guard at the Deaf club. I cannot be open there.
>
> (A Deaf lesbian, 1989)

All of the Deaf gay and lesbian people we interviewed complained that they could not express themselves in the open in the Deaf clubs because of the attitude of other members of the Deaf community. Many felt a pressure to deny their sexuality if they wanted to have any degree of acceptance in the Deaf club:

> What I don't like to see is when they kiss in front of people, in open public. I don't like to see that sort of behaviour happen in Deaf Centres.
>
> (A Deaf woman, 1989)

A commonly held belief amongst the Deaf people we interviewed was that gay and lesbian people are sexual predators, that all their social encounters are sexually motivated, and that they are a danger to the Deaf community. They are the 'Sexually Dangerous Other':

> Straight Deaf people think that gay people have nothing but sex, sex, sex, all the time.
>
> (A gay Deaf man, 1989)

> … when they go from one to another to me they are just the same as prostitutes.
>
> (A Deaf woman, 1989)

> I've got concerns about being approached by a gay person, I worry about being approached.
>
> (A Deaf man, 1989)

We were told by Deaf gay and lesbian people that they always 'put up a front' when in the Deaf club, and had to remain discreet. There is always a barrier between themselves and other Deaf people because many Deaf people do not want to meet with gay and lesbian Deaf people:

> If a gay or lesbian person came in and I didn't know they were gay or lesbian, fine, I would accept them, but if I found out they were gay or lesbian, then I would have strong objections to them coming in.
>
> (A Deaf man, 1989)

2.6.2 Being banned

A series of motions was tabled at the British Deaf Association's (BDA) Congress of 1987 to ban gay and lesbian Deaf people from the BDA. The 'anti-gay' groups were forced to withdraw their proposals and the BDA adopted the following resolutions:

> The BDA is totally opposed to sexism and racism in all their forms and to discrimination against disabled people, lesbians and gays.
>
> (*British Deaf News*, 1987)

Despite this declaration by the BDA, we encountered a high level of feeling amongst the Deaf people we interviewed that gay and lesbian Deaf people should be banned from the Deaf community. Even those who did not specifically advocate banning wanted to enforce stringent control measures:

> They should be banned. People should go in a clean way, nice husband and wife. Gays and lesbians are dirty, it shouldn't be. Just split them up, everything clean, make people clean. Then there's bisexuals, then with men and then they go with the women, I think that's worse, that's awful, it's dirty.
>
> (A Deaf woman, 1989)

> If they do something awful the committee could ask them to leave and ban them.
>
> (A Deaf man, 1989)

> We have the right to actually ban them ... perhaps ban them for three to six months and if they behave/improve let them back. We would not encourage them, it gives the town a bad name, I want to keep this town clean. I want it good and strict, we don't want awful things happening here.
>
> (A Deaf man, 1989)

A high percentage of the Deaf people interviewed spoke of 'banning' as a device for controlling gay and lesbian Deaf people in their Community. We do not know how often banning was used against gay and lesbian Deaf people, although we were given a number of examples, but many of the gay and lesbian Deaf people we interviewed felt that there was a form of covert banning, or internal isolation, practised quite widely:

> ... then people started to realize that they were gay and say, you know, it's awful, it's dreadful, it's shameful ... and then they just melted away really, they just dropped out.
>
> (A Deaf woman, 1989)

> ... sometimes maybe there would be a fight in the Deaf club because he was gay and some people wouldn't like it if they'd hear he was homosexual. So he started mixing more with hearing people ... and withdrew from the Deaf community.
>
> (A Deaf man, 1989)

> I saw quite a lot of coloured men (sic) and now the numbers have gone down because they were coloured Deaf gay people and people started to know who they were and they stopped coming, quite a lot of people stopped coming because they felt ashamed that people knew who they were and they actually left the club and just left it back with the normal people.
>
> (A Deaf man, 1989)

The gay and lesbian Deaf people we interviewed have largely opted out of the Deaf community in favour of their own support groups and the hearing gay community. Many gay Deaf people refer to Gay Sign Language (GSL) as a means of communication that they have developed amongst themselves. This should not be confused with British Sign Language (BSL), neither can it be considered a language. It is a collection of signs that gay and lesbian Deaf people have devised in order to maintain a measure of confidentiality when communicating with each other. Conversations in Deaf clubs, for example, can be easily watched by others. GSL is also used to establish the sexual orientation of people gay and lesbian Deaf people meet. Certain phrases act as a code so that lesbians and gays can recognize each other without others knowing. The fact that they refer to this communication as GSL is not an attempt to establish it as a language to compete with BSL (GSL users are first and foremost BSL users), but by naming it as such they are making a political point to the majority of the Deaf community about their own difference and separateness:

> Gay Sign Language is really like slang. There are no signs for things such as tables and chairs, it is more used to describe behaviour and feelings. It started so that straight Deaf people wouldn't know what we were talking about, it was sort of underground. But it's very important for us, we use it a lot amongst ourselves.
>
> (A gay Deaf man, 1990)

> We don't bother to teach our language to straight Deaf people because I'm sure they don't really want to be involved with us. In everyday life they're not going to use it, so why teach it to them? If straight Deaf people learnt GSL we would change it again. We'd disguise it so they couldn't work out what it was.
>
> (A gay Deaf man, 1990)

> I think GSL is limited compared with BSL, it's more like a code really. If both worlds were equal (gay-Deaf and straight-Deaf) we'd use the one language. But they aren't equal, so it's necessary for us to have GSL and to keep ahead of straight Deaf people, because it's safer and better for us in the gay Deaf world.
>
> (A gay Deaf man, 1990)

This feeling of disconnection from the Deaf world is also extended to the social workers who work with Deaf people:

> With our group, confidentiality is important. Gossip can spread around very quickly, that is why we are a bit careful about talking to Social Workers with the Deaf.
>
> (A Deaf lesbian, 1989)

> Some social workers will read the file and then go and tell other people.
>
> (A gay Deaf man, 1989)

We do not know how widespread this feeling is amongst gay and lesbian deaf people, but it was universal amongst those we interviewed.

The controversial Clause 28 of the Local Government Act 1988 actively discourages positive attitudes to homosexuality, on the basis that it will encourage homosexual development in young people. Bancroft (1988) asserts that any government wishing to reduce the amount of homosexual activity should support the notion of sexual equality, as 'homosexuality is more likely in those societies that strongly reinforce sex role stereotypes'.

The combined effect of rejection by the Deaf community and institutional rejection by social workers locates gay and lesbian deaf people firmly in the category of the 'Other'.

Now return to the questions we asked you in the first ITQ on page 7–8.

Would you answer the questions in the same way now in respect of lesbian and gay deaf people? If not, try to identify what it is that has caused you to alter your view. If your answers are broadly similar to those you came up with at the beginning, try and think of some new information which you have now, but did not have at the beginning, or some facet of the debate which you had not taken into account. Make some notes and keep them for Activity 4 at the end of this unit.

3 Deaf-blind people

We just want people to know that we are normal human beings that need that little bit extra help. We can make our own decisions but we need help for day-to-day things.

(A deaf-blind woman, 1989)

The above quotation comes from a meeting we had with a group of deaf-blind people. We had originally arranged to interview two or three deaf-blind people individually because we had assumed that a group interview

Figure 4.7   Deaf-blind people: a holiday abroad
(Source: National Deaf-Blind League, 1988)

would be very difficult, if not impossible—clearly a measure of our prejudice rather than of their capabilities. The group was self-selecting and there was an even number of men and women. Each deaf-blind person had a sighted/hearing person with them to interpret.

◄ Reading
You should now read Article 22 'How I live with Deaf-Blindness' by Patrick Murphy in Reader One. Patrick Murphy's personal account of being deaf-blind raises many of the issues dealt with in this section. ◄

3.1 Prevalence of deaf-blindness

There are no accurate figures relating to numbers of deaf-blind people. Klemz (1977) estimates that there are about 2,000 deaf-blind people in the UK, Lysons (1984) about 5,000. The Deaf-Blind Services Liaison Group (DBSLG), in their report *Breaking Through* (1988), estimate not less than 11,000 deaf-blind people in the UK. Yoken (1979) cites a Federal Government estimate of 21,000 deaf-blind children and adults in the USA. The DBSLG report states that anecdotal evidence would suggest that, in the London Boroughs, ten in every 200,000 people are recognized as deaf-blind, whereas the evidence from the small amount of research that has been undertaken places the estimate at five times that number.

On this basis the estimated deaf-blind population of the USA would be in excess of 56,000, whilst that of the UK would be approximately 13,000. There is no evidence to suggest that the incidence of deaf-blindness is significantly different in the two countries, so the comparison is reasonable. The US estimate of 21,000 is a Federal Government figure, whereas in the UK there is no official category of deaf-blind within the statistics gathered by the Department of Health. However, despite the difference in the means by which figures are arrived at, there does appear to be a serious underestimation of the actual number of deaf-blind people in both countries by the official agencies.

3.2 The deaf-blind community

'Deaf-blind' as a term does not adequately describe the different needs and experiences of the people to whom it is applied. The DBSLG report arrived at this working definition:

> ... persons are regarded as deaf-blind if they have a severe degree of combined visual and auditory impairment resulting in problems of communication, information and mobility.

> (DBSLG, 1988)

ITQ
Before proceeding, consider the following question:

What might be the important differences between someone who is born deaf and later loses his or her sight, and someone who is born blind and later loses his or her hearing?

Make a note of your answer before reading further.

Helen Keller commented that blindness cuts you off from things, whereas deafness cuts you off from people. To be deaf-blind by this analysis, then, would appear to be totally isolating. Without trying to minimize the effect of being deprived of both hearing and sight, the impact will vary depending upon life experience prior to the loss. For example, a deaf person who later in life loses his or her sight will be accustomed to a visual mode of communication, possibly sign language, and so would find the practical aspects of a transition to the deaf-blind manual (finger spelling on the hand of a deaf-blind person) relatively straightforward. An oral deaf person, reliant upon lip-reading, may experience more difficulty with this transition. A blind person who later loses his or her hearing, however, will probably have spoken language skills, and will be able to continue to use this form of expression. He or she will also be able to continue to use Braille without any difficulties.

The DBSLG report recognizes that deaf-blind people do not constitute a homogeneous group, and whilst a manageable definition of the term deaf-blind was necessary for the report, this definition in fact includes a range of people who will have experienced their deafness and blindness in very different ways, and, to a certain extent, their needs will be determined by the cause of their deafness and blindness and by the age of onset.

The National Deaf-Blind League (NDBL), in their 1988 report, divide the Deaf-Blind community into four main groups:

1 The person who loses sight and hearing in adult life (who will possess speech).

2 The blind person who subsequently loses hearing (who will also possess speech).

3 The deaf person who subsequently loses sight (who may be without speech).

4 The person deaf and blind from birth (who may also be without speech).

(National Deaf-Blind League, 1988)

The vast majority of people in Groups 1 and 2 are older people whose sight and hearing are failing with advancing years. Those in Group 3 are more likely to suffer from Usher syndrome, and those in Group 4 as a result of congenital rubella.

Rubella is a preventable disease and the vaccination is available free to girls over the age of 10 years and to women of child-bearing age. However, whilst statistics are gathered by the government, these only apply to a very narrow age group and it is not possible to use them to gauge satisfactorily the effectiveness of the school vaccination programme. This seems strange when one considers the virulence of rubella during pregnancy: in the rubella epidemic of 1963–1965, the incidence of rubella as a cause of deafness rose to 10 per cent of all those born deaf (Bordley and Hardy, 1969). Fifty per cent of those infants affected had heart disease, 50 per cent had hearing loss, 40 per cent had glaucoma or cataract, and 40 per cent had psychomotor retardation (Cooper et al., 1969).

Many of those children born with heart defects die in early infancy and their struggle is simply one of survival. The others are likely to be affected by more than one disability, with deafness more commonly present (68 per cent of children affected during the first trimester of pregnancy, 40 per cent during the second trimester, but deafness can result from rubella infection during any stage of pregnancy) (Bordley and Hardy, 1969). In the UK there is no need for doctors to inform the Registrar General of the numbers of cases of rubella they treat as, unlike many other countries, rubella is not a notifiable disease.

Usher syndrome has been estimated to affect three in 100,000 of the general population (Hallgren, 1959; Kloepfer *et al.*, 1966), and to be the most common cause of deaf-blindness, affecting 3 to 4 per cent of all children born deaf (Vernon, 1969). It is a recessive genetic disorder characterized by a hearing loss present at birth combined with gradually deteriorating eyesight caused by retinal degeneration, retinitis pigmentosa (RP, or sometimes commonly known as tunnel vision).

There are two very important features of Usher syndrome: (i) it is only found amongst congenitally Deaf people; and (ii) RP is usually not diagnosed until early adulthood.

The effects of Usher syndrome are usually chronic rather than acute. The rate of retinal degeneration is difficult to predict, and children in whom the disease has not been diagnosed may be assumed to be clumsy if they bump into things, or intellectually slow if they fail to receive the information they need at school and fall behind their classmates. Early diagnosis is vital and, as all sufferers of Usher syndrome are congenitally deaf, then schools for the deaf would appear to be the ideal places to develop screening and support services.

Creagh Walker-Day (1982) surveyed residential schools for the deaf in the USA to find out if they had screening procedures for Usher syndrome and what support was available. Of the forty schools (68 per cent) that took part in the survey, 33 per cent screened annually, 19 per cent every 3 years, and 19 per cent on request. Eighty-four per cent of those diagnosed as having Usher syndrome were over 12 years old (51 per cent were 16 years and older), and only 51 per cent of those schools with a screening procedure had any form of post-diagnostic support.

A British survey conducted by SENSE (the National Deaf-Blind and Rubella Association) (Guest and Roper, 1988) was an attempt to discover the numbers of diagnosed pupils in full-time education. Their survey revealed that the majority of pupils were aged 11 to 18, with a predominance of those diagnosed at around 16 years of age. However, whilst the eldest was 23 years old, there were also two 5-year-olds, and the report concludes that this demonstrates that diagnosis does not have to wait until adolescence.

The SENSE report revealed high levels of concern amongst teachers about two factors:

1   Teachers had insufficient clinical information regarding the vision of their deaf pupils. The test for RP is quite specific and it is not easily picked up by a routine eye test. Furthermore, the technicians administering the eye test are usually not sufficiently experienced in testing deaf people; for example, they will attempt to communicate verbally in a darkened room.

2   Many teachers reported that they had been refused permission by the parents to tell the child of his or her diagnosis. The report concludes that parents either could not communicate with their children or had not come to terms themselves with their child's diagnosis. The question must be raised as to what kind of support is available to parents in this situation.

With continuing education policy of integration, and the attendant closure of more residential schools for deaf children, surveys such as this will be much more difficult to conduct in the future and thus early diagnosis of Usher syndrome even more problematic to make.

3.3 Deaf-blind people and the Deaf community

We discussed the question of deaf-blindness with all the groups we interviewed for this unit, and the picture that emerged is that deaf-blind people are viewed with some sympathy by the Deaf community but are, nevertheless, isolated from it.

We began the discussion with this statement: 'Some people say that to be deaf-blind is a terrible personal tragedy, and there is nothing that anyone can do to help'. We invited the different groups to consider the statement, and to give us their own views. Everyone thought that it was a terrible personal tragedy, but their response as to whether deaf-blind people can be helped was divided into two recognizable categories:

> They are quite happy by themselves. Sometimes they will sit in a circle together talking on each other's hands, but usually I think they prefer to sit alone.
>
> (A sighted Deaf man, 1989)

The view expressed in the above quotation is one that a number of people considered to be accurate. These were mostly Deaf people who could not claim any personal acquaintance with deaf-blind people, but had seen them, perhaps in the Deaf club. They were also mostly men, and we will return to this point of gender-specific behaviour below.

The second major response was that deaf-blind people received quite a lot of help really, for which they were grateful, and with which they were reasonably content:

> We help them here, members and others, they help, yes they do help. We have deaf-blind holidays and they are quite happy with them. Hearing people help, and volunteers; it is very good. For born deaf-blind it is easier and they are quite happy with their lot in life, but if you suddenly go blind it can be a shock at a late age. But they know if they are born deaf-blind then they will be like it for life, so it's easier for them.
>
> (A sighted Deaf woman, 1989)

> We have a lot of deaf-blind here, mostly on Sunday for church. They enjoy their lives I think.
>
> (A sighted Deaf woman, 1989)

People who supported this view had either first-hand experience of deaf-blind people, or attended a club where there was a facility for deaf-blind people organized by social workers. The examples given to us of situations in which Deaf people had directly offered assistance to a deaf-blind person were very few and mostly some time ago. The respondents in this category were almost exclusively female, which leads us to speculate that gender-specific behaviour is a major contributory factor.

Acquaintance with deaf-blind people by Deaf men was much more likely to be from a distance, whereas acquaintance by Deaf women was almost always practical and of a personal contact nature. This is consistent with traditional socially constructed gender roles, with women being conditioned to be carers and practical helpers, whilst men are allocated supervisory or leadership roles.

Only one person offered an alternative view. A young Black Deaf man told us:

> It's the wrong attitude, it's really the wrong attitude. Whenever we do have a deaf-blind person in the Deaf centre, people really don't bother to help, they leave that person alone and I think that is a serious problem. It reminds me of an incident where I introduced a girl who was losing her hearing as well as her eyesight. I brought her into the Deaf centre and tried to get her to talk, but Deaf people didn't bother with her. Then there's Harry who's deaf-blind, he comes in, and Gill who's suffering from Usher syndrome. I try to talk to them, and take them around the club to talk to other people, because otherwise they are just left to sit by themselves with nobody to talk to. It's just not right.
>
> (A young Black Deaf man, 1989)

Figure 4.8   Deaf club members in conversation with a deaf-blind person
(Source: courtesy of the British Deaf Association)

We put the statement that '... to be deaf-blind is a personal tragedy and there is nothing that anyone can do to help' to the group of deaf-blind people. Their response was very clear:

> The statement you read out to us is the very attitude we are trying to fight against. It is the reason deaf-blind people are left out of things at Deaf clubs, because people think there is nothing they can do other than leave them sitting.
>
> (A deaf-blind woman, 1989)

Their experience of attending Deaf clubs was very negative:

> I can only say that in my time I was the only person who was deaf-blind to go to the Deaf club in my home town. I do not think it is right for deaf-blind people to go to Deaf clubs because they will be left out and left quiet. It is better for them to go to a deaf-blind club.
>
> (A deaf-blind man, 1989)

> That was my experience also, I went to Deaf clubs and was never included in the activities. I think what they do is too sight oriented, you cannot really join in their activities.
>
> (A deaf-blind woman, 1989)

> The guide would take me to the Deaf club, then leave me alone whilst they went off to talk to others. I was left there until it was time to go to the pub.
>
> (A deaf-blind man, 1989)

> I used to go to the day centre where I lived and there was a Deaf club down there every Friday night. I was put in touch with them but they did not think it would be any good because of my sight problems. They said I needed to be with deaf-blind people, but in my town I didn't know anybody else. I wanted to meet with other deaf people and use sign language but the Deaf there didn't want to bother. The staff at the day centre were keen to help but they had lots of other people to deal with.
>
> (A deaf-blind man, 1989)

> When I went to the Deaf club in my area I found that I was not accepted. I would be introduced to deaf people who would say that they had to go and do something right now but they would come and talk to me later—they never did.
>
> (A deaf-blind man, 1989)

The central theme running through the information given us by deaf-blind people was very clear: they had made a number of attempts to include themselves in the activities of Deaf clubs and had been met with rejection and isolation. This was regardless of whether the deaf-blind person was born deaf-blind, born deaf and later became blind, born blind and later became deaf, or born hearing and sighted later to become deaf-blind. The significant factor was that the treatment they received did not appear to be affected by their previous body image/sensory identity. If this is the case throughout the Deaf community, and we have no reason to believe it is not, then the future for those Deaf people with Usher syndrome would appear to be rather bleak, characterized by diminishing social contacts and isolation while they are still amongst people with whom they may have been friendly for many years.

The nature of the 'Otherness' of deaf-blind people in the Deaf community would appear to be that they are the 'Other' to be avoided, to be ignored. But is it more complex than that? Goffman (1968) describes the way in which 'stigmatized' people develop strategies in their encounters with 'normals', and in which the 'stigmatized' are expected to take responsibility for managing the encounter. Higgins (1980) states that encounters between deaf people and hearing people are characterized by deaf people having to adapt to the assumptions of hearing people in order to maintain the interaction as '*nothing* unusual is happening', or manage the interaction because '*something* unusual is happening'.

The relationship between Deaf people and deaf-blind people is that of the 'something unusual is happening' variety, and the claim by deaf-blind people that they are ignored and avoided by Deaf people is something that Deaf people experience in relation to hearing people. Goffman, however, asserts that the 'stigmatized' are labelled as deviant by 'normals', and are the subject of anger, criticism and blame. This is certainly not a feature of the relationship between Deaf people and deaf-blind people we have interviewed.

There may be a number of reasons for this—we identify two. First, society generally is reasonably well disposed towards blind people in a sympathetic, patronizing way. This is not unlike the attitude we found amongst Deaf people and it may be that their attitude simply reflects the general view of society towards blind people. Second, and perhaps more likely, is that there is an increased awareness amongst Deaf people about the impact of blindness on someone with a hearing loss. Deaf people operate in a visual medium and any interruption of that is serious because it threatens every aspect of their lives. It could be that being with deaf-blind people raises for them too many fears and anxieties about their own future. When one considers the relatively late onset of blindness caused by Usher syndrome, and the general deterioration of eyesight in old age, the prospect of being without hearing and sight at some point in their lives must be much more keenly felt amongst Deaf people than amongst hearing people.

One Deaf person told us:

> I know someone, a woman I used to go to school with. I hadn't seen her for a while and when I met her again I was shocked to see she was blind. It really frightened me, what can we do when we become blind?
>
> (A Deaf woman, 1989)

3.4 Services

Yoken (1979) refers to deaf-blind people in the USA as the 'invisible minority'. This is even more true in the UK, where, not only are statistics not gathered by the government, there is also no legal definition of deaf-blindness and no Acts of Parliament that deal specifically with the needs of deaf-blind people. Service providers usually rely upon Government Acts and statistical information to provide the incentive to develop their service profiles. The 1970 Chronically Sick and Disabled Persons Act did have a section which directed local authorities to inform themselves of numbers of deaf-blind children in their areas and make educational provision for them, if possible, in state schools. However, this part of the Act was never implemented and it was repealed in 1981. Deaf-blind people are expected to fit into the services provided for deaf people or blind people, a fact that dismays many deaf-blind people and those who work with them. One person in the interview group said:

> I went to a Deaf school for a year when I first came out of hospital and they were quite unable to teach me. They had no idea what approach to take. I couldn't speak, I couldn't lip-read, I couldn't read the blackboard, I couldn't read their text books, they were quite lost. Then I went to blind school and they were able to spare the time to give me individual tuition ... but I was still unable to join in with the rest of the class.
>
> (A deaf-blind woman, 1989)

The DBSLG report made comprehensive recommendations, which would locate the responsibility for services with local authorities in collaboration with voluntary agencies. The recommendations range from identifying numbers of deaf-blind people, through multidisciplinary assessments and self-advocacy schemes, to the implementation of training and support packages for staff in residential homes and hospitals. It remains to be seen whether any of these recommendations will be realized in action by central or local government.

The deaf-blind people we interviewed were in agreement with the need for an over-arching strategy for services, as recommended in the DBSLG report, and they produced their own list of the ten most important needs of deaf-blind people, as compiled by the deaf-blind consultant to the National Deaf-Blind League, Patrick Murphy. These needs are:

1   Education
2   Rehabilitation
3   Interpreters
4   Guides
5   Social intercourse
6   Public awareness
7   Responsibility
8   News and information
9   Daily living skills
10 Hobbies

They had concerns at different levels about services. About education they raised the issue of a need for more specialist teachers because education for deaf-blind children is most effectively achieved with one-to-one teaching. A further concern was *where* to educate deaf-blind children:

> Whether to integrate or educate them separately is an important issue. Deaf-blind children need to begin education very early, but do you send the child away from its parents at the age of three to go to a residential school, or leave them at home with their parents and lose the early training?
>
> (A deaf-blind woman, 1989)

The area of services about which they felt most strongly was that concerning social workers, guides and interpreters. The confusion of the roles of social workers and interpreters is ever present in the Deaf community generally, and to a certain extent this is also true for deaf-blind people. (This issue will be discussed in more detail in Unit 7.) But, although they identified social workers/guides/interpreters as being extremely important, they clearly wished to be in control of their own lives and were therefore very anxious about the quality of any relationship they might have with these people:

> I think what we need is a true, trustworthy friend, at least one. Somebody that understands and doesn't get impatient.
>
> (A deaf-blind man, 1989)

> Not someone who is paid because it might not be the right person. It should always be a true friend.
>
> (A deaf-blind man, 1989)

> A paid guide is not as true a friend as someone who is not paid. Social workers are paid and I have found some social workers that I do not like. They do not know how to help deaf-blind people.
>
> (A deaf-blind man, 1989)

> Very often social workers get the idea that because they have been trained they are perfect, and that, of course, is not true. They still have to learn how a deaf-blind person wants them to do things. We all have our likes and dislikes, so I would prefer a friend to a social worker.
>
> (A deaf-blind woman, 1989)

But the subject also raised a number of fears that perhaps altruism alone may not be sufficient to provide for their needs, and that some formalized arrangement might also be necessary.

> Although, a paid person could be more reliable perhaps because if they do not do what they are supposed to do they would not get paid.
>
> (A deaf-blind woman, 1989)

Figure 4.9 'Interpreting to the deaf-blind'
(Source: courtesy of the Royal National Institute for the Deaf)

There are times when to have paid help can be a great advantage. I am thinking more about interpreters than a guide, you want to go to a conference or a meeting where you need an interpreter and it is good to be able to ask someone to do it and offer to pay them. I feel it is asking a lot to expect them to finger spell for a whole day, for love.

(A deaf-blind woman, 1989)

This area of personal help highlights the vulnerability of deaf-blind people because, regardless of how intelligent, clear-thinking and physically active they may be, they are dependent upon the assistance of another person in order to do many of the things that hearing/sighted people take for granted. Their concern is for high levels of trust rather than for professional skills or expertise. By their attempts to be involved in Deaf clubs, deaf-blind people are clearly reaching out to the Deaf community with the hope of establishing trusting relationships. The position of deaf-blind people as the 'Other' to be avoided and ignored in Deaf clubs would seemingly militate against these relationships developing:

At the Deaf club Deaf people are involved in many different activities. It is true that deaf-blind people cannot join in all of them, but a Deaf person could tell us what was happening. Then we would have some choice and could make more of a contribution.

(A deaf-blind woman, 1989)

ITQ
Now return to the questions we asked you in the first ITQ on page 7–8.

Would you answer the questions in the same way now in respect of deaf-blind people? If not, try to identify what it is that has caused you to alter your view. If your answers are broadly similar to those you came up with at the beginning, try and think of some new information which you have now, but did not have at the beginning, or some facet of the debate which you had not taken into account. Make some notes and keep them for Activity 4 at the end of this unit.

---

4 Older deaf people

The past is a foreign country: they do things differently there.

(L.P. Hartley, *The Go-Between*)

Figure 4.10   Older deaf people in conversation
(Source: courtesy of the British Deaf Association)

4.1 Images of older people

There are two popular images of old age. One portrays older people as lonely, sad and depressed. The other portrays them as free of the day-to-day demands of society, employment and family responsibilities and thus able to pursue a full range of enjoyable activities. Both views, however, run the risk of being little more than simple stereotypes. The experience of old age depends largely upon social class, education and financial status. Those who have acquired wealth during their working lives stand a greater chance of enjoying a fruitful and comfortable old age than those people dependent upon state benefits. This does not mean that older people on state benefits cannot enjoy a fruitful and comfortable old age, simply that it may be more difficult for them to achieve, as the state benefit system fails to relate pensions to realistic living costs. As Thomson asserts:

> Elderly dependents from the 1830s to the 1870s received from their communities cash allowances with value equivalent to two-thirds or more of the incomes of non-aged working class adults. It has been accepted in the present century (by contrast) that the elderly (in Britain) should be given little more than one-third of the resources of other adults.

(Thomson, in Fennell *et al.*, 1988)

In *The Sociology of Old Age*, Fennell *et al.* (1988) discuss a number of different theories as to why elderly people are marginalized in British society. They quote Townsend, who argues that there is a clear link between 'income and social participation', and that poor people in a society which values 'buying power' will find themselves outside of the main area of social activity and their needs will be considered least. This dissonance will be highlighted only by specific events which may accidently identify some previously hidden social need. An example of this is the way in which some older people are unable to afford railway travel other than at times of special concessions or offers, and this goes largely unnoticed. Their desire to travel by rail is not diminished by the fact that it is beyond their financial capability, and surfaces wherever conditions allow:

> British Rail introduced a special 'day return to anywhere' concession to pensioners (in 1980 and 1984). The 1980 scheme promoted the biggest wave of mass travel since the evacuee trains of the Second World War. Nearly one million pensioners bought tickets, some travelling from Scotland to Cornwall and back.
>
> (Bornat *et al.*, in Fennell *et al.*, 1988)

General social trends in post-war Britain have led to a separation between people of different ages and social classes. Ethnic minorities in cities tend to congregate in particular areas, likewise, social services departments focus most of their activities upon particular council estates, and the more affluent members of society tend to live amongst people who are most like themselves. Younger people moving out of city centres leave older people where they are, and with city centre regeneration, offers of rehousing to older people usually mean sheltered housing, residential provision, or warden-controlled accommodation, rather than the opportunity to live in mixed communities.

As the gulf between the different social groups has widened in recent years, those people in social minority groups (older people, unemployed people, people with physical and mental handicaps, and single parent families, for example) are finding that they are increasingly less well off, despite a general rise in the standard of living. For example: 'As car ownership becomes more common and public transport declines, those without a car become actually and relatively worse off in terms of accessibility and in what they have to pay for transport' (Fennell *et al.*, 1988).

There are a number of theories which attempt to explain the marginality of older people in society. Disengagement theory was developed in the 1950s by a group of social gerontologists at the University of Chicago. This implies that society makes fewer demands upon individuals as they grow older, and, in turn, the individual enjoys and encourages this withdrawal from involvement. It appears, therefore, that this process of disengagement permits the older person increased freedom from the constraints and norms controlling everyday behaviour. To what extent the older person actually exercises this freedom may depend upon the reaction of family and friends who still feel they need to 'conform'.

A process of change is occurring with respect to older people and there is some reduction in their social activity: Disengagement theory does not take into account social factors which act upon older people, forcing them to withdraw from a variety of social situations. The unequal power relationships which exist within our society put elderly people in a vulnerable position, particularly in respect of employment, from which retirement ages are predetermined and take no account of the physical well-being or the competence of individuals (unless they happen to be directors of multinational companies, or members of the House of Lords, or judges).

In Role theory, the marker for the end of a man's working life is the point at which he will withdraw and disengage from general social activity. For women, this marker is widowhood. The central assumption that underpins this theory is that work is the most important social role for men and marriage for women. Retirement from either of these institutions initiates a process of role diminution, resulting in a loss of status and a feeling of functionlessness. According to Role theory, this has the effect of reducing levels of involvement in all social situations.

The withdrawal from social situations leads to social isolation and it is this isolation that, according to Role theorists, poses the greatest challenge to older people. It is not, they argue, financial hardship which marginalizes older people. Although loss of the work role in a society driven by the protestant work ethic has a significant impact, it cannot by itself explain the marginalization experienced by older people, and we would contend that financial hardship must be taken into account. Townsend, in his study amongst older people in Bethnal Green (Townsend, 1957), recognizes that changing social roles and status have an effect upon the lives of older people, but by far the most significant factor is the sudden drop in income.

A Social Construction approach puts forward the social organization of labour and structural inequality as the major influences on the lives of older people, and not the ageing process. As Townsend states:

> Retirement, poverty, institutionalisation and restriction of domestic and community roles are the experiences which help to explain the structured dependency of the elderly. [In this analysis it is] society [that] creates the framework of institutions and rules within which the general problems of the elderly emerge or, indeed, are 'manufactured'. In the everyday management of the economy and the administration and development of social institutions the position of the elderly is subtly shaped and changed. The policies which determine the conditions and welfare of the elderly are not just the reactive policies represented by the statutory social services but the much more generalised and institutional policies of the state which maintain or change social structure.
>
> (Townsend, in Fennell *et al.*, 1988)

4.2 Older people in the Deaf community

Are the general attitudes of society towards older people replicated in the Deaf community? The Deaf community was described in the Introduction by one of its members as '... just like a family really'. We wanted to find out how the 'Deaf family' was treating its older members.

In our discussions with the various groups within the Deaf community we gained the impression that they are generally well disposed towards older people, and expressed concern for their well-being and financial difficulties:

> A lot of older Deaf people out there have got complaints and problems, and they're always with the social workers over problems with their flats and food and everything. It's really hard for them, just affording food; there's a lot of problems. Some people have got their work pension, and some just don't have anything; it ought to be 50/50, it should be the same for both, or just a little bit different, but it's really not fair.
>
> (A Deaf woman, 1989)

> I sometimes meet old people, it's quite interesting when they talk about when they were young, years ago, and they were looking forward to being adults. They tell me that when they were working it was fine, they had plenty of money, and eventually as they got older, 50, 55, 60, then it was really hard to find work. When you are 60 it's different because some hearing people carry on working when they are 60 and find other jobs, but that's impossible for a Deaf person, and I've seen old Deaf people getting upset about that.
>
> (A Deaf man, 1989)

Despite the generally benign attitude towards older deaf people expressed by the majority of Deaf people we interviewed, the day-to-day experience of older deaf people was at variance with this view:

> Some of the Deaf ignore people because they're old, some do. Because of that I don't come as often as I did.
>
> (An older Deaf man, 1989)

> We were on the committee of the social club ... when it was the AGM the young people used to say, 'We don't want the old people, we'd rather have young people on it'.
>
> (An older Deaf woman, 1989)

> They just ignore the old, they just stick together, the young ones. All the old ones are happy together, when the young ones come it's different. I think the club ought to be split into two, with a room for the young ones and a room for the old ones.
>
> (An older Deaf man, 1989)

Many of the older Deaf people we interviewed said that what they experienced was a diminished role within the Community; they were reduced to observing many of the club activities rather than participating in them. They had, almost all of them, been heavily involved in club activities in the past, as committee officials, or as voluntary tutors to younger people, and had generally been involved in Community affairs. From a position at the centre of Community life, their role is now so peripheral that, for the most part, they have scant knowledge of developments in their own Community.

Older Deaf people felt they had a contribution to make to Community life which was not being recognized or acted upon. They were sad that the wealth of their experience was not being used to good effect by younger deaf people. They have lived through many changes in educational and social policies, and participated in many developments in the Deaf community, and believe that their knowledge would be of benefit to younger deaf people:

> When I was young, and we were with old people, I liked it because you could get information and things from them. I don't agree with the club being split, I think we should all be together. They can pick things up from old people. When I was 16 and 17 I used to go with the old ones on trips, I used to really enjoy being with them. Some of the old people would complain, 'Oh! It's awful, she's watching us talking'. And someone else would say, 'No, no, it's not that at all, she's actually picking up information, she's not spying'.
>
> (An older Deaf woman, 1989)

46

Their views are often not invited, even when they themselves are significantly affected by the decision being made:

> These changes in the club here, we have had a new building in the front, there is a dark room. There are no windows. Us old ones, we feel a bit upset about it. We feel like we are in a prison. Before it was all windows and we could see everybody walking past. It was light and we could play cards and look out, now it is dark. We have lost all interest in the club now.
>
> (An older Deaf woman, 1989)

The oldest and longest serving member of that Deaf club told us:

> There are a lot of differences now ... I miss the light from the windows.
>
> (An older Deaf woman, 1989)

 ◀ Reading
You should now read the following articles in Reader One in which Deaf people remember the Second World War and Tom and Jack remember their schooldays. Older Deaf people are a rich source of stories, a living history, of which this is a small sample:

Article 32, 'Memories of a War' by George Taylor;

Article 33, 'Memories of a School' by George Taylor. ◀

Figure 4.11   Royal Cross School, Preston
(Source: courtesy of the Royal National Institute for the Deaf)

4.3 Services

Marginalization and isolation are problems encountered generally by older people in society. For an older deaf person the isolation can be even more stark. Deaf people are scattered in society, and sometimes the local Deaf club is the only point of contact with other deaf people. Older deaf people, often living alone, may not be able to communicate with their neighbours, and may live some distance from their local Deaf club.

Community support services for older people offered by social services departments are often not appropriate for Deaf people. Home helps, where they receive any training at all about hearing impairment, usually learn about hard-of-hearing people, and lack an understanding of the needs of profoundly Deaf people. Local authority day-centres for older people are likewise not geared up to assist older Deaf people, who may remain as isolated in the day-centre as they do in their own home.

Similarly with residential care: there are a small number of independently run residential homes specifically for older Deaf people, but they are few and far between. The majority of older deaf people who require residential provision rely upon local authority provision. But are local authority homes for older people suitable places for older Deaf people?

ITQ

What extra considerations would need to be taken into account when providing residential accommodation for older Deaf people? Make a list of the elements you consider to be important before reading further.

A survey conducted in 1987, in one particular local authority, looked at that authority's residential provision for older people to see how suitable it was for older Deaf people.

Figure 4.12   Older Deaf people in a residential unit
(Source: courtesy of the Royal National Institute for the Deaf)

Of the twenty homes in the survey, with a total of 276 care staff, only four members of staff had any knowledge of manual communication, but they were not employed in the homes where the Deaf sign language users lived. Although there were over 100 hearing aid users across all the homes, only four homes had a loop amplifier system, and two of these homes were unsure whether the system worked or how to test it.

Nine homes had leaflets on how to cope with deafness, but staff felt that these were dated and they were generally unused. There was even less information available for the residents: most stated that the printed matter was for staff use only. Only two homes had teletext televisions, yet all of them knew of subtitling. None of the homes made use of the RNID play synopsis facilities available at that time.

Most serious of all, however, was the fact that none of the homes had any visual fire alarm system, yet most admitted that the majority of their residents would not hear a fire bell. No one knew how many sign language users were living in the residential homes, just that there were some—but these people were by themselves without access to others with whom they could communicate effectively.

Being isolated in this way is acutely felt by older Deaf people who will probably have developed a network of Deaf friends stretching back to their schooldays. The residential school system means that Deaf people have strong links with their contemporaries for a long time after they leave school. (The changing nature of educational provision threatens these community links for future generations of Deaf people.)

Most Deaf centres have some provision for older Deaf people to meet with each other, but this is usually focused around bingo or a luncheon club, where older Deaf people are separated from other Deaf people in the Club, something which disturbed many of the older Deaf people we interviewed. Whilst older Deaf people want to participate on equal terms in Deaf clubs, they are viewed by younger Deaf people as 'past their prime'. They are the recipients of sympathy and patronage, their 'Otherness' is informed by the notion that they have little or no contribution to make to the modern Deaf community; their decision-making powers have been subtly removed from them, and their needs are identified as being simply recreational:

> Our needs are the same as other Deaf people, but sometimes we're treated like children by the younger ones. What they don't understand is that we have experienced many of the problems they have, and we could help them.
>
> (An older Deaf man, 1989)

ITQ

Now return to the questions we asked you in the first ITQ on page 7–8.

Would you answer the questions in the same way now in respect of older deaf people? If not, try to identify what it is that has caused you to alter your view. If your answers are broadly similar to those you came up with at the beginning, try and think of some new information which you have now, but did not have at the beginning, or some facet of the debate which you had not taken into account. Make some notes and keep them for Activity 4 at the end of this unit.

---

5 Oral deaf people

My teacher told me that I will have to mix with hearing people if I want to get on in the world, so I will have to be able to speak to them. That is why I don't want sign language.

(A young Deaf man, 1989)

◄ Reading
This would be an appropriate point at which to read about the history of oralism in the Set Book *British Sign Language: A Beginner's Guide* by Miles, pp. 25–6. ◄

5.1 Who are oral deaf people?

So far we have been discussing Deaf people who are marginalized because of some unalterable quality, which places them in the category of the 'Other'. Oral deaf people, provided they are white, heterosexual, young and sighted, would appear to be in a somewhat different position. Their 'Otherness' comes from their inability or unwillingness to sign and their real or perceived attitudes towards the Deaf community.

There are a number of reasons why some deaf people do not use sign language. These are reflected in the two main groups of oral deaf people:

1   Some oral deaf people choose not to belong to the Deaf community and prefer to live and work in the hearing world on hearing terms.
2   Social Workers with Deaf People tell us that in some areas there is an increasing number of young deaf school leavers, educated in an oral system, who are struggling within the hearing world yet do not feel any affiliation with the Deaf world.

There is a further group of deaf people who are able to use speech but can also communicate in sign language. Their capacity to be bilingual often means that they occupy a specific place in the Deaf community. They are not 'oral deaf' in that they are also sign language users, but some of the issues that surround them are pertinent in this section.

◄ Reading
We would like you now to read three Reader articles as a preparation for this section. They are all from Reader One.

Article 10, 'Making Plans for Nigel: The Erosion of Identity by Mainstreaming' by Paddy Ladd (which you also read in conjunction with Unit 2);

Article 11, 'Life at Secondary School' by Elizabeth Craddock;

Article 12, 'A Polytechnic with a Difference' by Lucy Briggs. ◄

5.2 Oral deaf people and the Deaf community

Higgins (1980) comments on what he calls 'the cleavage between signers and speakers'. He states that 90 per cent of the Deaf community of the USA are signers, whilst the other 10 per cent are speakers, and the split between them is almost a formal arrangement. The Deaf clubs of Chicago are a typical example of this. Where at one time signers and speakers met in the same building, although in separate groups, they now have separate buildings. Each group is uncomfortable in the other's presence and with the other's mode of communication.

According to Higgins, the conflict between signing and speaking can also have a major disruptive effect on family life. Deaf people, even in the same family, educated according to different communication regimes, may find their relationship strained. Given that the vast majority of deaf children are born into hearing families, the implications of this are quite profound. The following are just some of the issues to which this situation gives rise:

—Saul N. Kessler

INSTEAD OF TRYING TO TEAR DOWN THE WALL OF DEAFNESS, WHY NOT TRY THE DOOR?

Figure 4.13
(Source: courtesy of the Royal National Institute for the Deaf)

1 How do deaf children become socialized into the Deaf community?
2 Can they become truly bicultural or do they fall between two cultures, belonging to neither culture fully?
3 Do they leave behind their hearing/speaking 'family culture' and adopt the cultural mores of the Deaf community?
4 Where can this socialization into the Deaf way of life take place and who is responsible for it? Is it the responsibility of the school or the parents or the Deaf community to 'induct' the young deaf into the Community?

It may be argued that it is not the responsibility of schools to socialize deaf children into the Deaf community; that the cultural values of any child, hearing or deaf, are best developed within the child's home. The situation for deaf children is more complex than it is for hearing children, however. Hearing children are usually well grounded in their home culture and grow out from it through school into the adult world.

What happens to deaf children born into hearing families? What cultural base will be established for them? And if they are to have a choice of a hearing and a Deaf culture, where will they gain access to Deaf culture?

One of the reasons the Deaf community objects to the closure of schools for the deaf, and one of the reasons for the passionate arguments behind the introduction of BSL into the classroom, is that many Deaf people believe that schools for the deaf play an important part in the generation and maintenance of Deaf culture.

Are schools the best places for inculcating a sense of community, self-identity and belonging in pupils—particularly pupils who represent a minority community? Or are the assertions of Deaf people that Deaf history remains untaught and devalued correct? And that schools for the deaf run by hearing people have a long history of trying to repress Deaf language and culture?

> The ethos of schools for the Deaf until very recently has become that the use of Sign Language would prevent the children from acquiring language and speech. Although this view is no longer held in the majority of schools there are still some teachers and some establishments, especially training establishments for teachers of the deaf, who still adhere to these views.

> (Royle, 1986)

(You will already have come across the issue of education and the Deaf community in your work on Unit 2, where it is explored in Section 5.2.)

There have been positive changes during the 1980s in attitudes towards the use of sign language within schools and some teachers are committed to the use of sign language as an educational tool. However, even in schools where sign language is accepted it is used mostly by hearing teachers, many of whom have poor signing skills themselves.

Many teachers are still 'psychologically oralist': they do not use sign language because they value it or the Deaf community, but merely tolerate signs to support the teaching of English. The pupils do not have access to the true language of Deaf people and are thus denied access to the sophisticated nuances and features of BSL. Signed English rather than BSL is therefore the medium of schools.

The employment of Deaf adults within schools for the deaf is limited. The reasons given for this are, for example, that their qualifications in English are not suitable, their speech is not clear, and they have no experience of working in schools. It may be that no Deaf people applied for the job in question, but one would then need to ask where the post was advertised. Was it advertised in a form accessible to Deaf people—for example, on videotape in a Deaf Centre, or on a Deaf programme such as *No Need to Shout* or *Earshot?*

◀ Reading
Now read Article 19 'A Deaf Teacher: A Personal Odyssey' by Janice Silo in Reader One, where the author describes the difficulties faced by a Deaf person who wants to become a teacher. ◀

When Deaf adults are employed in schools they hold minor positions—pupils do not often see Deaf adults in high status roles. How then can the pupils acquire a good self-image and a positive identity as Deaf individuals? In such a situation, how and where are Deaf young people expected to acquire the social and linguistic skills that the adult world expects from them?

Higgins (1980) states that signing is a prerequisite for membership of the Deaf community, and those who cannot sign find it difficult to become fully accepted, as lack of signing is seen as a lack of commitment to the Deaf world. Signing is bound up in notions of self and group identity, it is the outward badge of membership of the Deaf community, and those Deaf people who do not sign are viewed as outsiders.

In Unit 2 you looked at a definition of the Deaf community that based the Community on shared experiences which are expressed in a shared language. Those who do not sign efficiently may miss out on community

Figure 4.14 'Teaching the dumb (*sic*) to speak'
(Source: courtesy of the Royal National Institute for the Deaf)

life. Deaf people who speak and do not sign, for example, are singled out as collaborators who are seeking to join the dominant hearing and speaking world and who reject their Deaf identity.

The Deaf groups we interviewed expressed a very clear preference for being with other signers. They either did not know any oral deaf people and did not know where they socialized —

> Perhaps they go into town and drink in the pubs there. They don't come here. I mean, they can talk so they like hearing people better than me.
>
> (A Deaf man, 1989)

> There aren't any here. Only people who can sign.
>
> (A Deaf woman, 1989)

— or, they expressed a strong resistance to oral Deaf people coming into the Deaf club:

> We can't stop them. If oral people want to come they can come. We can't stop them.
>
> (A Deaf woman, 1989)

> Would they like it if I went to an oral club? I could be oral if I wanted to because both my parents are hearing on both sides. But it is not for me.
>
> (A Deaf man, 1989)

Although banning was never mentioned, as with some groups, the message was sometimes quite explicit:

> ... communication is the important thing. If you do not use the same method—sign language—you will be excluded.
>
> (A Deaf woman, 1989)

> I don't agree with oral deaf people. If they are born deaf then they should sign. No, I don't want oral people. NO THANK YOU.
>
> (A Deaf woman, 1989)

Amongst the Deaf signers we interviewed there were two general categories of opinion regarding oral deaf people. These two categories relate to the different groups of oral deaf people described at the beginning of this section, although the Deaf people in the interview groups did not specifically identify them as such. The two categories of opinion are:

1   That oral deaf people are somehow subversive, and undermining of the Deaf community:

> They think like hearing people ... Well, they are embarrassed to be Deaf and use sign language in the streets.
>
> (A Deaf woman, 1989)

> I met an oral deaf guy. I brought him to the club to make friends and he just withdrew and followed me around. 'What's wrong?' I said, 'I don't like people signing,' he said, 'I don't like it.' He had no patience, he had no interest in signing. I didn't want to know. No. I didn't want to know. I've heard that he goes to an oral deaf club where he can meet people.
>
> (A Deaf woman, 1989)

You teach them and teach them but they don't want to know.

(A Deaf man, 1989)

Perhaps they don't want to come, because they don't like signing.

(A Deaf woman, 1989)

I've got a cousin—he is deaf. He was at —— school. He is really clever. He doesn't sign. He is oral.

(A Deaf woman, 1989)

2   That oral deaf people are to be pitied as they are isolated and are victims of the education system:

If they don't go to the Deaf club where will they go for amusement?

(A Deaf man, 1989)

I see Deaf people signing and I like it that way. I see the oral group and their faces are solemn. You've got signing people laughing and oral people really glum. You tell a joke or something and the oral people can't pick it up ... signing people laughing ... the oral deaf people just ...

(A Deaf woman, 1989)

I met a man, he was oral. He wasn't very happy.

(A Deaf woman, 1989)

In our research we did not encounter a Deaf signer who believed oral deaf people to be his or her equal, although some Deaf signers thought that oral deaf people considered themselves to be superior to other Deaf people.

Higgins (1980) cites the work of Furth and Jacobs who stated that post-lingually deafened people, who speak intelligibly and sign, generally received a better education and are more likely to occupy leadership positions in the Deaf community. Higgins states that these people are not 'leaders' in the true sense but rather those who have assumed important positions within the Community. They seek to act on behalf of other Deaf people and have taken on the mantle of spokespeople and mediators between the Deaf and hearing worlds.

He argues that although these people claim to speak for the Deaf community they are not held in high regard by the rest of the Community. Many are thought to be snobbish and self-regarding. It is felt that they use their educated status to try and dominate the less well educated Deaf people and disregard them as inadequate. There is much resentment towards these 'college educated' Deaf people which is expressed in the signs used by the other Deaf people:

They criticize such college educated Deaf by mockingly referring to themselves with a variation of the sign for 'college'. By inverting the sign, literally turning it upside down, it can be used sarcastically to criticize those who, in the words of a Deaf man, 'think they are high'. Translated into English, the inverted sign for 'college' means 'so you think you are smart; well I am just uneducated, the opposite of college educated'.

(Higgins, 1980)

Many of these educated oral deaf people do not go to the Deaf clubs, although some do and may mix freely with and marry into the non-college community. However, the shared experience of deafness does not totally transcend the barriers created by educational difference.

In this country social class may also be a contributory factor in this 'cleavage' between the orally successful and the signing Deaf communities. The selective schools (Mary Hare and Burwood Park) for deaf children have been most staunchly oral and produce the largest numbers of deaf people with qualifications. Rodda stated in his work that: 'Children receiving selective special education are drawn from economically superior groups', and also that: 'Selective special schools take children with a lower average loss and at a later onset of deafness than other types of special school' (Rodda, 1970).

We interviewed some young deaf people who had received an oral education, not in selective schools for deaf children but in Partially Hearing Units (PHUs). Whilst one or two of them did use a few signs, their preferred mode of communication was through speech and lip-reading. We asked their views on sign language and the Deaf community, and where they felt they belonged. Although severely deaf from birth, their response was overwhelmingly that they considered themselves to be hearing people:

> With hearing people I learn a lot, and I like to go out with them.
>
> (A young deaf man, 1989)

> Most people understand me when I speak.
>
> (A young deaf man, 1989)

> I don't like sign language because hearing people say it doesn't matter.
>
> (A young deaf man, 1989)

> I like to talk to hearing people. I'll find a girlfriend one day, a hearing girlfriend.
>
> (A young deaf man, 1989)

Although, when pressed further, there were some indications of uncertainty and confusion for some:

> Really I can't say which is best. Well, I feel partly in the Deaf world and partly in the hearing world. I mostly want to be with hearing people.
>
> (A young deaf man, 1989)

> I can't learn signing, I can't read, can't understand, not very well. I can't read and I can't write.
>
> (A young deaf man, 1989)

> At my school there was no signing, nothing at all. It was oral. I mean, we used to sign in secret. Why couldn't I have learnt more at school?
>
> (A young deaf woman, 1989)

> School? Oh, yes. It was oral. No signing at all. If you signed you got the stick.
>
> *Did they hit you?*
>
> Oh, yes. If they saw you signing, that was it! It was all speech. Oral.
>
> (A deaf man, 1989)

These young people were not only confused about where they belonged but were very restricted in their use of language. They could not communicate their thoughts and views—either in English or in BSL. It appeared that the education system had failed to meet their linguistic needs.

Many deaf young people leave school with a generally low level of educational attainment. There has been an overemphasis on language issues, and the content of the curriculum has been subjected to arguments over the mode of instruction (Unit 5 deals with educational issues in more detail):

> Deaf children throughout their development are likely to evidence an increasing gap between what they know, think and feel on the one hand, and what they can express, negotiate and communicate about on the other. This growing gap between knowledge and communication often dislocates processes of social interaction, teaching and learning.
>
> (Wood *et al.*, 1986)

Under the current evaluation system, many young deaf people enter the adult world ill-prepared and at a distinct social and educational disadvantage. They have limited access to general knowledge about the world at large and a poor understanding of career possibilities. They do not 'overhear' other people talking about jobs and the variety of opportunities is lost to them. Access to books, television and other media is restricted by their communication levels and mode.

Residential schools cocoon the young people and isolate them from the outside world. There is restricted access to the community (Deaf and hearing) outside the school boundaries. Integrated mainstream schooling and the provision made by PHUs isolate young deaf people from each other. The young people experience language deprivation and cultural disadvantage. Even in PHUs where signing is allowed, the number of deaf people is small and the age range is often quite wide, providing a restricted peer group. There is no real sign language community to nourish and develop their communication skills beyond the superficial and mundane:

> We have a duty to try to determine whether the spoken language that a deaf child might acquire extends below the surface skin of the exchange of facts and into the texture of thought.
>
> (Conrad, 1979)

The young deaf adults we interviewed certainly found it difficult to give structure and texture to their thoughts. They appeared to be ill at ease and experiencing a low sense of self-worth. It seemed as if they had become detached from the markers against which they could measure themselves as people. The hearing world's markers are inappropriate—they know they are different—but the Deaf world is also inaccessible. They are the 'Other', the pariah in both worlds.

How can the gap between the expectations of the community at large (Deaf and hearing) and the reality of the young oral deaf people be bridged? This task is often undertaken by Social Workers with Deaf People and groups such as Friends of the Young Deaf. One social worker who undertakes group work with these young people told us:

There is a need for an on-going group for profoundly and severely deaf young adults, providing social skills, information, discussion and an opportunity to improve the self-image of people who have had an inadequate oppressive education and who see themselves as grossly inferior to their hearing peers. All the members that attended the oral education system believe strongly that to speak is superior to sign. That to learn and to rely on sign language was seen as a failure by the school and the teachers.

The young people feel that the sole responsibility for communication rested with themselves rather than the hearing people having to make any effort. They feel that the problem lies within themselves and see it as their responsibility to integrate into a hearing world rather than wanting to educate hearing people about deafness and Deaf people.

ITQ

Now return to the questions we asked you in the first ITQ on page 7–8.

Would you answer the questions in the same way now in respect of oral deaf people? If not, try to identify what it is that has caused you to alter your view. If your answers are broadly similar to those you came up with at the beginning, try and think of some new information which you have now, but did not have at the beginning, or some facet of the debate which you had not taken into account. Make some notes and keep them for Activity 4 at the end of this unit.

---

6 Conclusion

At the beginning of this unit we raised a number of questions concerning the relationships between different groups of deaf people. We said that these are groups which exist either formally or informally within the Deaf community, and that their relationships with each other will be mediated by notions of what it is to be a 'normal' Deaf person. This approach was chosen in order that the complexity of the Deaf community could be demonstrated from the perspective of its least powerful members. The notion of the 'Other' is useful here, it describes a way of organizing which is based on the values of the dominant group, and locates all 'Others' as hostile to, and outside of, those values.

 ◀ Activity 4
Now look back at the notes you made arising from the questions we set at the end of each section. Are there similarities between the answers for each different group? Or, is each group unique in the way that it relates to the majority Deaf community? As a final exercise, write your own brief summary of the ways in which the different groups looked at in this unit relate to each other, focusing on how they are similar to each other and how they are different, in the way they fit into the Deaf community. ◀

Unlike the hearing community, there is a notion that the Deaf community is closely knit, that is like a family and welcomes all Deaf members. However, the idea that 'The Deaf community is just like a family really, and all Deaf people are in it', is clearly not supported by most of the groups we interviewed. Why this is so is different for each group.

Many of the prejudices present in the hearing community also feature in the Deaf community. Thus, racism separates Black deaf people from white deaf people, and homophobia separates gay and lesbian deaf people from heterosexual deaf people. Both Black deaf people and gay and lesbian deaf people look more to the hearing community than to the Deaf community for their support. Gay and lesbian deaf people were almost universally vilified by the heterosexual Deaf people we interviewed, and their behaviour subject to much control. The situation is similar for Black deaf people— before they are made welcome they are expected to divest themselves of much of their cultural identity.

Oral deaf people find themselves outside of the Deaf community, but without a recognizable hearing group to which they can belong. They are viewed as not having sufficient commitment to the Deaf community because of their reliance on spoken language. Their position is, therefore, alterable, as long as they learn to use sign language, a straightforward reversal of the situation in which Deaf people normally find themselves.

In Section 3 you learnt how the attempts of deaf-blind people to be included in the Deaf community had met with rejection. We put forward a possible explanation for this—sighted Deaf people may have a heightened sense of awareness to the loss of sight which raises fears about their own future. Deaf-blind people represent these fears and they are therefore to be avoided.

Older people, on the other hand, appear to suffer the same fate in the Deaf community as in the hearing community. That is, people are generally well disposed towards them, but nobody takes them seriously. The effect of this is to put older deaf people at a significant disadvantage compared with their hearing counterparts. Older people have right to certain health and welfare services, very few of which are appropriately geared up for Deaf people, and Deaf community facilities tend to focus upon recreation.

The hostility implicit in the notion of the 'Other' was more evident in some cases than in others. Gay and lesbian deaf people were subjected to open hostility, and to a lesser extent so were oral deaf people. The insidiousness of racism, however, means that hostility is sometimes difficult to detect. The Black deaf people we interviewed were used to experiencing it and were able to be very clear. Deaf-blind people and older deaf people were viewed benignly by almost everyone we interviewed, but the consequence of their 'neglect' by the Deaf community considerably worsens their circumstances.

What is true of all these groups is that they felt some anger towards the majority Deaf community, and the phrase 'a bad attitude' was frequently used about the way they were treated. This was less so for older deaf people, many of whom had been members of the same club for many years. They had experienced something different in the past and, whilst they were unhappy about the way they were treated now, they were more prepared to accept it as inevitable.

It is easy to be critical of the Deaf community for the way it treats some of its members, but it is not surprising. Deaf people are an oppressed group, they are oppressed by the hearing majority who impress upon them that the cultures, values and languages of hearing people are important, and those of Deaf people are not. Oppressed groups closely observe their oppressors and know their conventions well. For example, Black people in Britain know more about white British culture than white Britains do about Black British culture. The way that Deaf clubs are organized is a result of the influence of many years of hearing missioners, social workers and members of the clergy. We can conclude that for some sections of the Deaf community this has not been helpful. Whilst some of the attitudes expressed by Deaf people in the interview groups are offensive and should be challenged, this does not mean that Deaf people are incapable of organizing their own community in a different way. The 'model' of dominance and leadership that Deaf people have is that of hearing people, along with its rules and prejudices.

As Freire writes:

> All domination involves invasion—at times physical and overt, at times camouflaged, with the invader assuming the role of helping friend … Cultural conquest leads to the cultural inauthenticity of those who are invaded; they begin to respond to the values, the standards, the goals of the invaders. In their passion to dominate, to mould others to their patterns and their way of life, the invaders desire to know how those they have invaded apprehend reality—but only so that they can dominate the latter more effectively. In cultural invasion it is essential that those who are invaded come to see their reality with the outlook of the invaders rather than their own; for the more they mimic the invaders, the more stable the position of the latter becomes.
>
> (Freire, 1972)

Suggestions for further reading

CHEETHAM, J., JAMES, W., LONEY, M., MAYOR, B. and PRESCOTT, W. (eds) (1981) *Social Community Work in a Multi-Racial Society,* London, Harper and Row in association with The Open University Press.
This is a collection of articles about the responses of the social and community services in Britain to the varied needs of ethnic minority groups.

FRYER, P. (1988) *Black People in the British Empire.* This book is an introduction to *Staying Power,* also by Peter Fryer, and gives an account of Britain's treatment of its colonial subjects since the twelfth century, which challenges the accepted white view of colonial history. Published by Pluto Press, London.

IGNATIEFF, M. (1990) *The Needs of Strangers,* London, The Hogarth Press. This book explores the difference between the fundamental need to survive and the *human* need to live as a person.

KOVEL, J. (1988) *White Racism,* Free Association Books.
This locates the roots of racism within social processes and the needs of individuals to externalize their negative characteristics.

References

ANDERSON, G.B. and BOWE, F.G. (1972) 'Racism within the Deaf community', *American Annals of the Deaf,* December, pp. 617–19.

BABUSCIO, J. (1988) *We Speak for Ourselves,* London, SPCK.

BANCROFT, J. (1988) 'Homosexuality: compatible with full health', *British Medical Journal,* vol. 297, pp. 308–9.

BORDLEY, J.E. and HARDY, J.M.B. (1969) 'Laboratory and clinical observations on pre-natal rubella', *Annals of Otology, Rhinology and Laryngology,* pp. 917–28.

BRIGGS, L. (1990) 'A polytechnic with a difference', in Taylor, G. and Bishop, J. (eds) (1990) *Being Deaf: The Experience of Deafness,* London, Pinter Publishers. (D251 Reader One, Article 12)

BRITISH DEAF NEWS (1987) *Editorial,* August.

CENTRE FOR CONTEMPORARY CULTURAL STUDIES (1982) *The Empire Strikes Back,* London, Hutchinson University Library.

CHARLES, A. and COOMBS, R. (1990) 'Growing up in care', in Taylor, G. and Bishop, J. (eds) (1990) *Being Deaf: The Experience of Deafness,* London, Pinter Publishers. (D251 Reader One, Article 24)

CLARK, D. (1987) *The New Loving Someone Gay,* Berkeley, CA, Celestial Arts.

CONRAD, R. (1979) *The Deaf School Child,* London, Harper and Row.

COOPER, L.Z., TRING, P.R., OCHERSE, A.B., FEDUN, B.A., KIELY, B. and KRUGMAN, S. (1969) in *American Journal of Disability in Children,* no. 18, p. 118.

CRADDOCK, E. (1990) 'Life at secondary school', in Taylor, G. and Bishop, J. (eds) (1990) *Being Deaf: The Experience of Deafness,* London, Pinter Publishers. (D251 Reader One, Article 11)

DE BEAUVOIR, S. (1988) *The Second Sex*, London, Picador. (First published in 1949.)

DEAF-BLIND SERVICES LIAISON GROUP (DBSLG) (1988) Report: *Breaking Through*, DBSLG.

FENNELL, G., PHILLIPSON, C. and EVANS, H. (1988) *The Sociology of Old Age,* Milton Keynes, The Open University Press.

FREIRE, P. (1972) *Pedagogy of the Oppressed*, London, Penguin Books.

FRYER, P. (1984) *Staying Power*, London, Pluto Press.

GOFFMAN, E. (1968) *Stigma*, Harmondsworth, Pelican Books.

GUEST, M. and ROPER, F. (1988) *Usher Syndrome in the School Population*, London, SENSE (The National Deaf-Blind and Rubella Association).

HAIRSTON, E. and SMITH, L. (1983) *Black and Deaf in America,* Maryland, T.J. Publishers, Inc.

HALLGREN, V. (1959) 'Retinitis pigmentosa combined with congenital deafness with vestibulo-cerebellar ataxia and mental abnormality in a proporation of cases. A clinical and geneticostatistical study', *Acta Psychiatrica Scandinavica,* Supplement no. 138, pp. 1–101.

HIGGINS, P. (1980) *Outsiders in a Hearing World*, Beverly Hills, CA, Sage Publications.

INSTITUTE OF RACE RELATIONS (1982a) *Roots of Racism*, London, Institute of Race Relations.

INSTITUTE OF RACE RELATIONS (1982b) *Patterns of Racism*, London, Institute of Race Relations.

KLEMZ, A. (1977) *Blindness and Partial Sight,* Cambridge, Woodhead-Faulkner.

KLOEPFER, M.W., LANGUATE, J.K. and MCLAURIN, J.W. (1966) 'The hereditary syndrome of congenital deafness and retinitis pigmentosa', *Laryngoscope*, vol. 76, pp. 850–62.

LADD, P. (1981) 'Making plans for Nigel: the erosion of identity by mainstreaming', in Taylor, G. and Bishop, J. (eds) (1990) *Being Deaf: The Experience of Deafness*, London, Pinter Publishers. (D251 Reader One, Article 10)

LYSONS, K. (1984) *Hearing Impairment,* Cambridge, Woodhead-Faulkner.

MILES, D. (1988) *British Sign Language: A Beginner's Guide*, London, BBC Books (BBC Enterprises). (D251 Set Book)

MURPHY, P. (1990) 'How I live with deaf-blindness', in Taylor, G. and Bishop, J. (eds) (1990) *Being Deaf: The Experience of Deafness*, London, Pinter Publishers. (D251 Reader One, Article 22)

NATIONAL DEAF-BLIND LEAGUE (1988) *Report*, Peterborough, National Deaf-Blind League.

NYMAN, D. (1990) 'A deaf-gay man', in Taylor, G. and Bishop, J. (eds) (1990) *Being Deaf: The Experience of Deafness,* London, Pinter Publishers. (D251 Reader One, Article 23)

RODDA, M. (1970) *The Hearing Impaired School Leaver*, London, London University Press.

ROYLE, P. (1986) Unpublished paper presented to NNEB working party, Basford Hall Council, Nottinghamshire.

SHEPHERD, S. and WALLIS, M. (eds) (1989) *Coming on Strong*, London, Unwin Hyman.

SILO, J. (1990) 'A deaf teacher: a personal odyssey', in Taylor, G. and Bishop, J. (eds) (1990) *Being Deaf: The Experience of Deafness*, London, Pinter Publishers. (D251 Reader One, Article 19)

TAYLOR, G. (1990) 'Memories of a war', in Taylor, G. and Bishop, J. (eds) (1990) *Being Deaf: The Experience of Deafness,* London, Pinter Publishers. (D251 Reader One, Article 32)

TAYLOR, G. (1990) 'Memories of a school', in Taylor, G. and Bishop, J. (eds) (1990) *Being Deaf: The Experience of Deafness,* London, Pinter Publishers. (D251 Reader One, Article 33)

TAYLOR, G. and BISHOP, J. (eds) (1990) *Being Deaf: The Experience of Deafness*, London, Pinter Publishers. (D251 Reader One)

TOWNSEND, P. (1957) *The Family Life of Old People*, Harmondsworth, Pelican Books.

VERNON, M. (1969) 'Usher syndrome: deafness and progressive blindness', *Journal of Chronic Diseases*, no. 22 , pp. 133–51.

WALKER-DAY, C. (1982) 'Current screening procedures for Usher syndrome at residential schools for the deaf', *American Annals of the Deaf*, vol. 127, no. 1, pp. 45–8.

WEEKS, J. (1977) *Coming Out*, London, Quartet Books.

WOOD, D.J., WOOD, H., GRIFFITHS, A. and HOWARTH, I. (1986) *Teaching and Talking with Deaf Children,* New York, Wiley.

YOKEN, C. (1979) *Living with Deaf-Blindness*, Washington, DC, The National Academy of Gallaudet College.

Acknowledgements

Grateful acknowledgement is made to the following sources for permission to reproduce material in this unit:

Figures
Figure 4.1 Institute of Race Relations (1982) *Roots of Racism. Book 1*; *Figure 4.2* Institute of Race Relations and Chris Abuk (1982) *Patterns of Racism. Book 2*; *Figure 4.3* The Mansell Collection; *Figure 4.5* Brenda Prince, Format; *Figure 4.6* Ray Hamilton, Camera Press; *Figure 4.7* The National Deaf-Blind League; *Figures 4.4, 4.8 and 4.10* The British Deaf Association; *Figures 4.9, 4.11, 4.12, 4.13, 4.14* The Royal National Institute for the Deaf.

Grateful acknowledgement is made to Trevor Landell for permission to use his painting on the covers and title pages throughout the units of this course.